THE 96 MOST IMPORTANT EUROPEAN PEINTERS OF ALL TIME

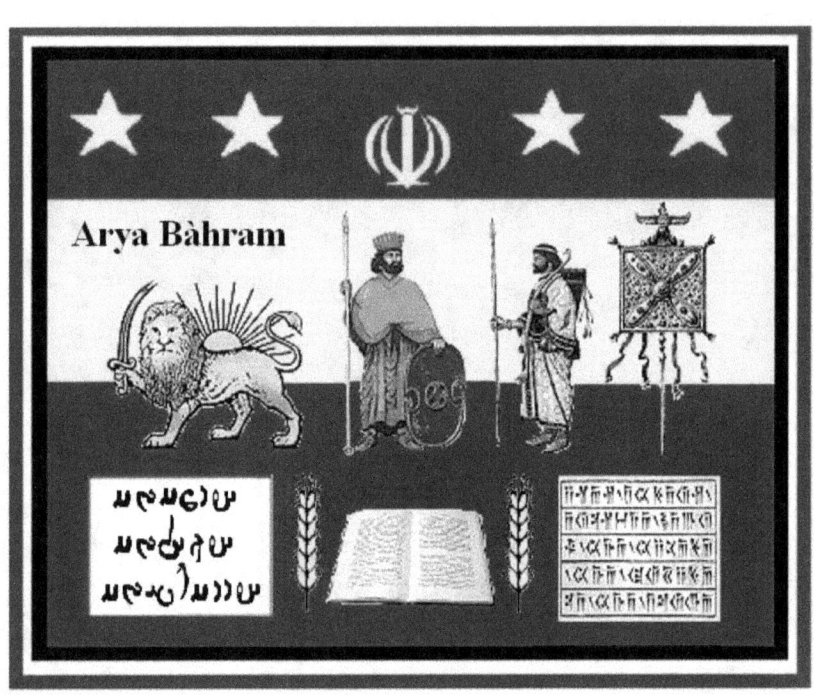

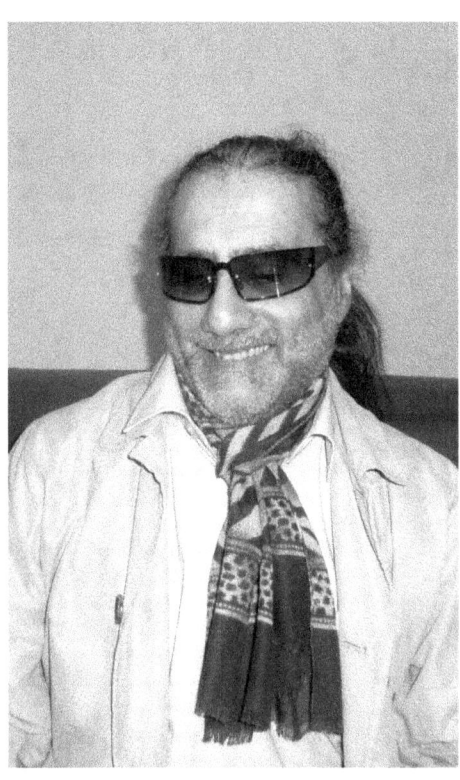

Do you know the most important European painters?
I am sure you have often heard a few names from them, But do you know how they looked?
Do you know which country these painters came from? When were they born and died?

I must say honestly, I have also not been able to answer many of these questions.
But this book gives you answers.
Have fun!

Connaissez-vous les plus grands peintres européens?
Je suis sûr que vous avez souvent entendu quelques noms d'eux, Mais connaissez-vous leurs visage?
Savez-vous de quel pays étaient ces peintres? Quand sont-ils nés et sont-ils morts?

Je dois dire honnêtement que je n'ai pas non plus réussi à répondre à bon nombre de ces questions.
Mais ce livre vous donne des réponses.
S'amuse bien!

Kennen Sie die wichtigsten europeaischen Maler?
Ich bin überzeugt, sie haben oft manchen Namen von ihnen gehört, aber wissen Sie wie sie ausgeschaut haben? Wissen Sie, aus welchem Land diese Maler kamen? Wann sie geboren und gestorben sind?

Ich muss ehrlich sagen, ich habe auch viele von diesen Fragen nicht beantworten können.
Aber dieses Buch gibt Ihnen Antworten
Viel Spaß!

painter	country
ALBRECHT DÜRER (1471-1528)	Germany
AMEDEO MODIGLIANI (1884-1920)	Italy
ARSHILLE GORKY (1905-1948)	Armenia
ARTEMISIA GENTILESCHI (1593-1656)	Italy
AUGUST MACKE (1887-1914)	Germany
AUGUSTE RENOIR (1841-1919)	France
BERTHE MORISOT (1841-1895)	France
CAMILLE COROT (1796-1875)	France
CAMILLE PISSARRO (1830-1903)	France
CASPAR DAVID FRIEDRICH (1774-1840)	Germany
CHARLES FRANCOISE DAUBIGNY (1817–1878)	France
CLAUDE LORRAIN (1600-1682)	France
CLAUDE MONET (1840-1926)	France
DANTE GABRIEL ROSSETTI (1828-1882)	England
DIEGO VELÁZQUEZ (1599-1660)	Spain
EDGAR DEGAS (1834-1917)	France
ÉDOUARD MANET (1832-1883)	France
EDVARD MUNCH (1863-1944)	Norway
EGON SCHIELE (1890-1918)	Austria
EL GRECO (1541-1614)	Greece
EUGENE BOUDIN (1824-1898)	France
EUGÈNE DELACROIX (1798-1863)	France
FERNAND LÉGER (1881-1955)	France
FRANCISCO DE GOYA (1746-1828)	Spain
FRANCISCO DE ZURBARÁN (1598-1664)	Spain
FRANS HALS (c.1580-1666)	Netherlands
FRANZ MARC (1880-1916)	Germany
FRIEDENSREICH HUNDERTWASSER(1928-2000)	Austria
GEORGES BRAQUE (1882-1963)	France
GEORGES SEURAT (1859-1891)	France
GIORGIO DE CHIRICO (1888-1978)	Italy
GIORGIONE (1478-1510)	Italy
GIOTTO DI BONDONE (c.1267-1337)	Italy
GUSTAV KLIMT (1862-1918)	Austria
GUSTAVE COURBET (1819-1877)	France

painter	country
GUSTAVE DORE (1832-1883)	France
GUSTAVE MOREAU (1826-1898)	France
HANS HOLBEIN THE YOUNGER (1497-1543)	Germany
HENRI DE TOULOUSE LAUTREC (1864-1901)	France
HENRI FANTIN LATOUR (1836-1904)	France
HENRI MATISSE (1869-1954)	France
HENRI ROUSSEAU (1844-1910)	France
HIERONYMUS BOSCH (1450-1516)	Netherlands
HONORE DAUMIER (1808-1879)	France
JACOPO TINTORETTO (1518-1594)	Italy
JACQUES LOUIS DAVID (1748-1825)	France
JAMES ENSOR (1860-1949)	Belgium
JAN GOSSEAERT (1478-1532)	Netherlands
JAN VAN EYCK (1390-1441)	Netherlands
JAN VERMEER (1632-1675)	Netherlands
JEAN ANTOINE WATTEAU (1684-1721)	France
JEAN AUGUSTE DOMINIQUE INGRES (1780-1867)	France
JEAN FRANÇOIS MILLET (1814-1875)	France
JEAN LEON GEROME (1824-1904)	France
JEAN SIMEON CHARDIN (1699-1779)	France
JOACHIM PATINIR (1480-1524)	Belgium
JOAN MIRÓ (1893-1983)	Spain
JOHN CONSTABLE (1776-1837)	England
JOSEPH MALLORD WILLIAM TURNER (1775-1851)	England
KAZIMIR MALEVICH (1878-1935)	Russia
LEONARDO DA VINCI (1452-1519)	Italy
LUCIO FONTANA (1899-1968)	Italy
MARC CHAGALL (1887-1985)	Russia
MARCEL DUCHAMP (1887-1968)	France
MAURICE QUENTIN DE LA TOUR (1704-1788)	France
MAURICE UTRILLO (1883-1955)	France
MAX ERNST (1891-1976)	Germany
MICHELANGELO BUONARROTI (1475-1564)	Italy
MICHELANGELO MERISI DA CARAVAGGIO (1571-1610)	Italy
NICOLAS POUSSIN (1594-1665)	France

painter	country
OSKAR KOKOSCHKA (1886 – 1980)	Austria
PABLO PICASSO (1881-1973)	Spain
PAOLO UCCELLO (1397-1475)	Italy
PAUL CÉZANNE (1839-1906)	France
PAUL GAUGUIN (1848-1903)	France
PAUL KLEE (1879-1940)	Switzerland
PETER PAUL RUBENS (1577-1640)	Netherlands
PIERRE BONNARD (1867-1947)	France
PIET MONDRIAN (1872 -1944)	Netherlands
PIETER BRUEGEL THE ELDER (1528-1569)	Belgium
RAPHAEL (1483-1520)	Italy
REMBRANDT VAN RIJN (1606-1669)	Netherlands
RENÉ MAGRITTE (1898-1967)	Belgium
ROGER VAN DER WEYDEN (1399-1464)	Netherlands
SALVADOR DALI (1904-1989)	Spain
SANDRO BOTTICELLI (1445-1510)	Italy
SIMONE MARTINI (1284-1344)	Italy
THEODORE GÉRICAULT (1791-1824)	France
TIZIANO VECELLIO (c.1476-1576)	Italy
TOMMASO MASACCIO (1401-1428)	Italy
UMBERTO BOCCIONI (1882-1916)	Italy
VINCENT VAN GOGH (1853-1890)	Netherlands
WASSILY KANDINSKY (1866-1944)	Russia
WILLEM DE KOONING (1904-1997)	Netherlands
WILLIAM ADOLPHE BOUGUEREAU (1825-1905)	France
WILLIAM BLAKE (1757-1827)	England

berühmte europaer (maler)	
Painter	**Country**
BLAKE WILLIAM (1757-1827)	England
BOCCIONI UMBERTO (1882-1916)	Italy
BONDONE GIOTTO (c.1267-1337)	Italy
BONNARD PIERRE (1867-1947)	France
BOSCH HIERONYMUS (1450-1516)	Netherlands
BOTTICELLI SANDRO (1445-1510)	Italy
BOUDIN EUGENE (1824-1898)	France
BOUGUEREAU WILLIAM ADOLPHE (1825-1905)	France
BRAQUE GEORGES (1882-1963)	France
BUONARROTI MICHEL ANGELO (1475-1564)	Italy
CÉZANNE PAUL (1839-1906)	France
CHAGALL MARC (1887-1985)	Russia
CHARDIN JEAN SIMEON (1699-1779)	France
CHIRICO GIORGIO (1888-1978)	Italy
CONSTABLE JOHN (1776-1837)	England
COROT CAMILLE (1796-1875)	France
COURBET GUSTAVE (1819-1877)	France
DA VINCI LEONARDO (1452-1519)	Italy
DALI SALVADOR (1904-1989)	Spain
DAUBIGNY CHARLES FRANCOISE (1817–1878)	France
DAUMIER HONORE (1808-1879)	France
DAVID JACQUES LOUIS (1748-1825)	France
DE KOONING WILLEM (1904-1997)	Netherlands
DE LA CROIX EUGÈNE (1798-1863)	France
DE LA TOUR MAURICE QUENTIN (1704-1788)	France
DEGAS EDGAR (1834-1917)	France
DORE GUSTAVE (1832-1883)	France
DU CHAMP MARCEL (1887-1968)	France
DÜRER ALBRECHT (1471-1528)	Germany
EL GRECO (1541-1614)	Greece
ELDER PIETER BRUEGEL (1528-1569)	Belgium
ENSOR JAMES (1860-1949)	Belgium
ERNST MAX (1891-1976)	Germany
FANTIN LA TOUR HENRI (1836-1904)	France

berühmte europaer (maler)	
Painter	**Country**
FONTANA LUCIO (1899-1968)	Italy
FRIEDRICH CASPAR DAVID (1774-1840)	Germany
GAUGUIN PAUL (1848-1903)	France
GENTILESCHI ARTEMISIA (1593-1656)	Italy
GÉRICAULT THEODORE (1791-1824)	France
GEROME JEAN LEON (1824-1904)	France
GIORGIONE (1478-1510)	Italy
GORKY ARSHILLE (1905-1948)	Armenia
GOSSEAERT JAN (1478-1532)	Netherlands
GOYA FRANCISCO (1746-1828)	Spain
HALS FRANS (c.1580-1666)	Netherlands
HUNDERTWASSER FRIEDENSREICH (1928-2000)	Austria
INGRES JEAN AUGUSTE DOMINIQUE (1780-1867)	France
KANDINSKY WASSILY (1866-1944)	Russia
KLEE PAUL (1879-1940)	Switzerland
KLIMT GUSTAV (1862-1918)	Austria
KOKOSCHKA OSKAR (1886 – 1980)	Austria
LÉGER FERNAND (1881-1955)	France
LORRAIN CLAUDE (1600-1682)	France
MACKE AUGUST (1887-1914)	Germany
MAGRITTE RENÉ (1898-1967)	Belgium
MALEVICH KAZIMIR (1878-1935)	Russia
MANET ÉDOUARD (1832-1883)	France
MARC FRANZ (1880-1916)	Germany
MARTINI SIMONE (1284-1344)	Italy
MASACCIO TOMMASO (1401-1428)	Italy
MATISSE HENRI (1869-1954)	France
MERISI DA CARAVAGGIO MICHEL ANGELO (1571-1610)	Italy
MILLET JEAN FRANÇOIS (1814-1875)	France
MIRÓ JOAN (1893-1983)	Spain
MODIGLIANI AMEDEO (1884-1920)	Italy
MONDRIAN PIET (1872 -1944)	Netherlands
MONET CLAUDE (1840-1926)	France
MOREAU GUSTAVE (1826-1898)	France

berühmte europaer (maler)	
Painter	**Country**
MORISOT BERTHE (1841-1895)	France
MUNCH EDVARD (1863-1944)	Norway
PATINIR JOACHIM (1480-1524)	Belgium
PICASSO PABLO (1881-1973)	Spain
PISSARRO CAMILLE (1830-1903)	France
POUSSIN NICOLAS (1594-1665)	France
RAPHAEL (1483-1520)	Italy
RENOIR AUGUSTE (1841-1919)	France
ROSSETTI DANTE GABRIEL (1828-1882)	England
ROUSSEAU HENRI (1844-1910)	France
RUBENS PETER PAUL (1577-1640)	Netherlands
SCHIELE EGON (1890-1918)	Austria
SEURAT GEORGES (1859-1891)	France
TINTORETTO JACOPO (1518-1594)	Italy
TOULOUSE LAUTREC HENRI (1864-1901)	France
TURNER JOSEPH MALLORD WILLIAM (1775-1851)	England
UCCELLO PAOLO (1397-1475)	Italy
UTRILLO MAURICE (1883-1955)	France
VAN DER WEYDEN ROGER (1399-1464)	Netherlands
VAN EYCK JAN (1390-1441)	Netherlands
VAN GOGH VINCENT (1853-1890)	Netherlands
VAN RIJN REMBRANDT(1606-1669)	Netherlands
VECELLIO TIZIANO (c.1476-1576)	Italy
VELÁZQUEZ DIEGO (1599-1660)	Spain
VERMEER JAN (1632-1675)	Netherlands
WATTEAU JEAN ANTOINE (1684-1721)	France
YOUNGER HANS HOLBEIN (1497-1543)	Germany
ZURBARÁN FRANCISCO (1598-1664)	Spain

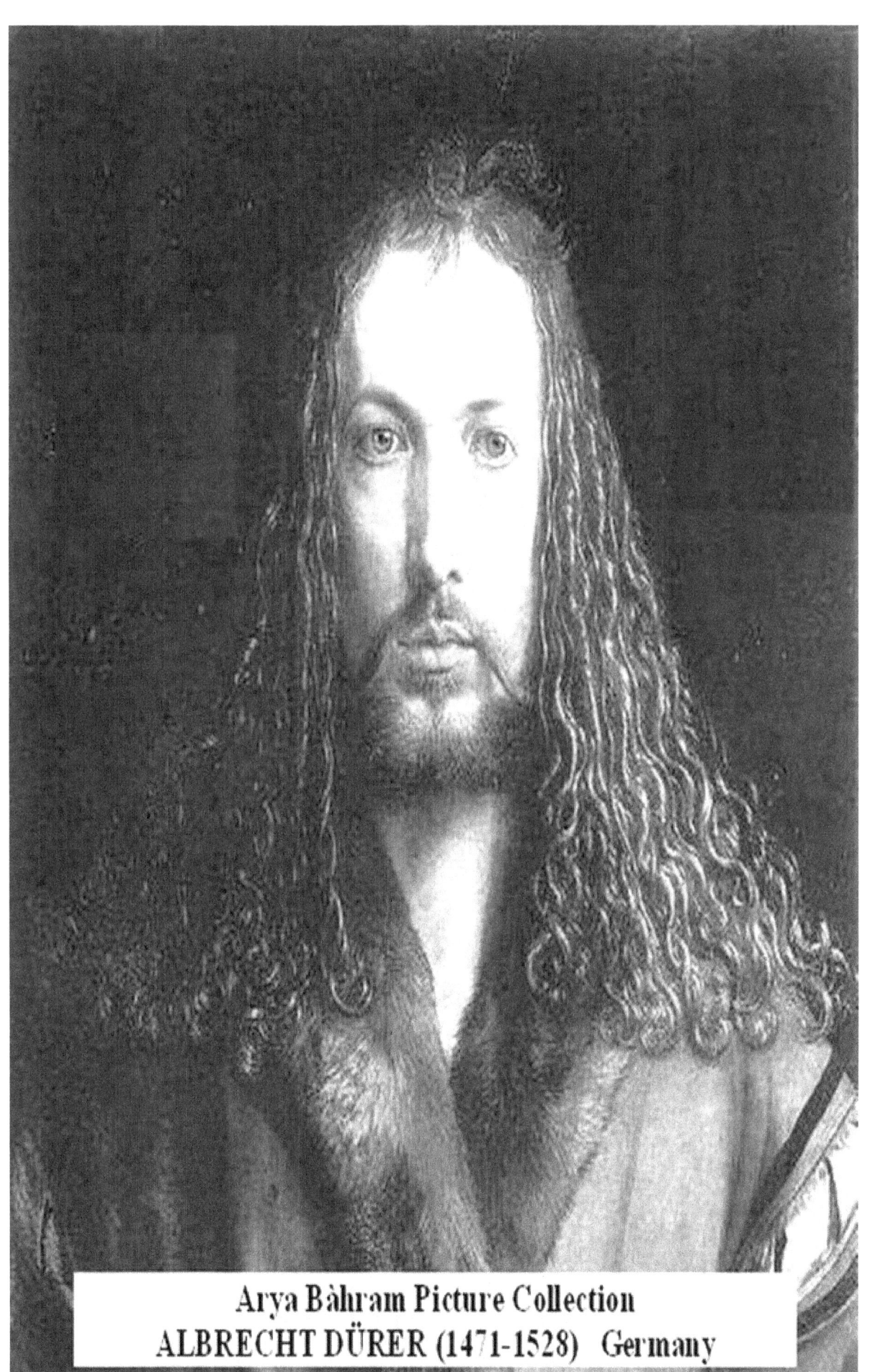

Arya Bàhram Picture Collection
ALBRECHT DÜRER (1471-1528)   Germany

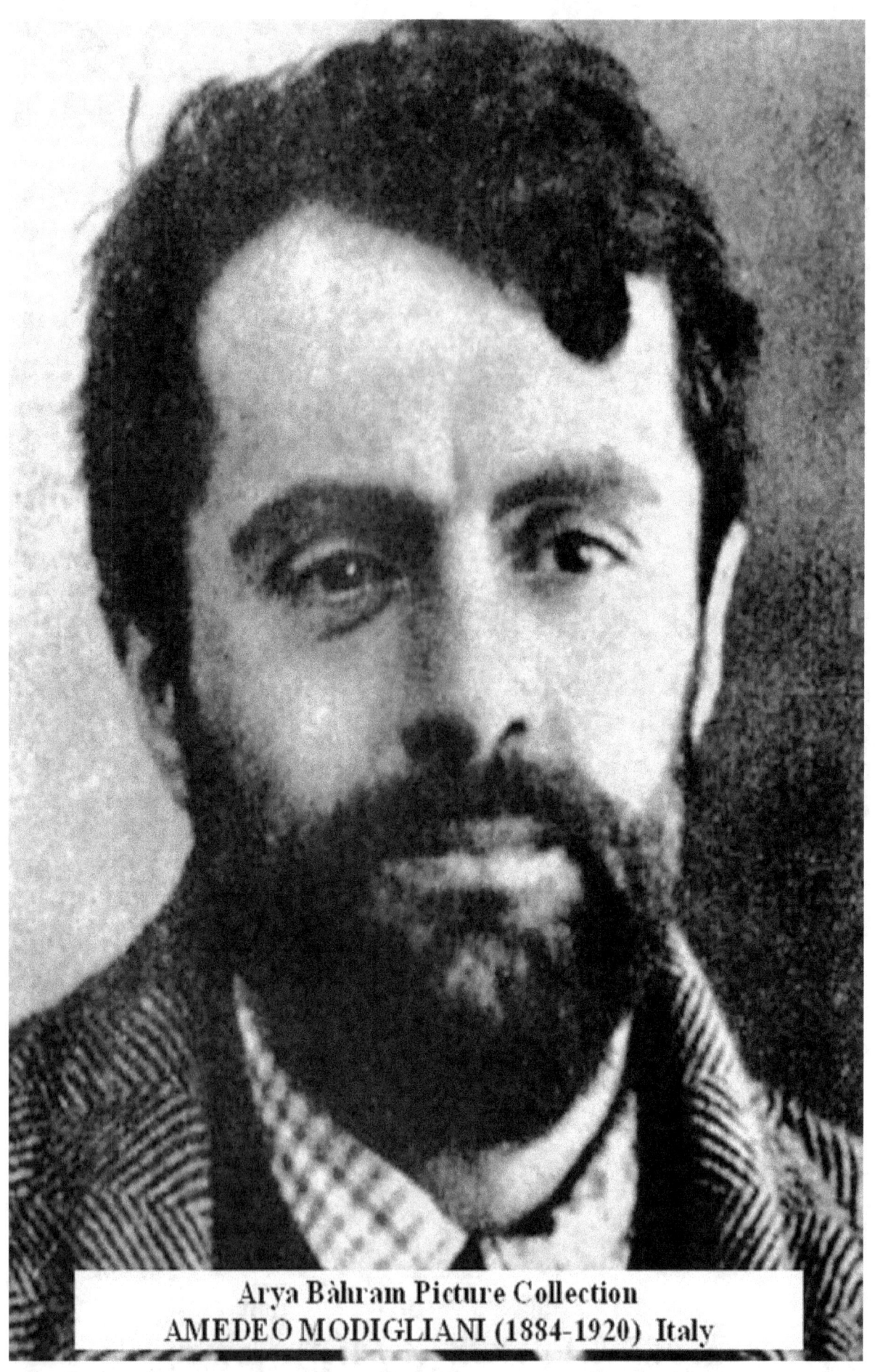

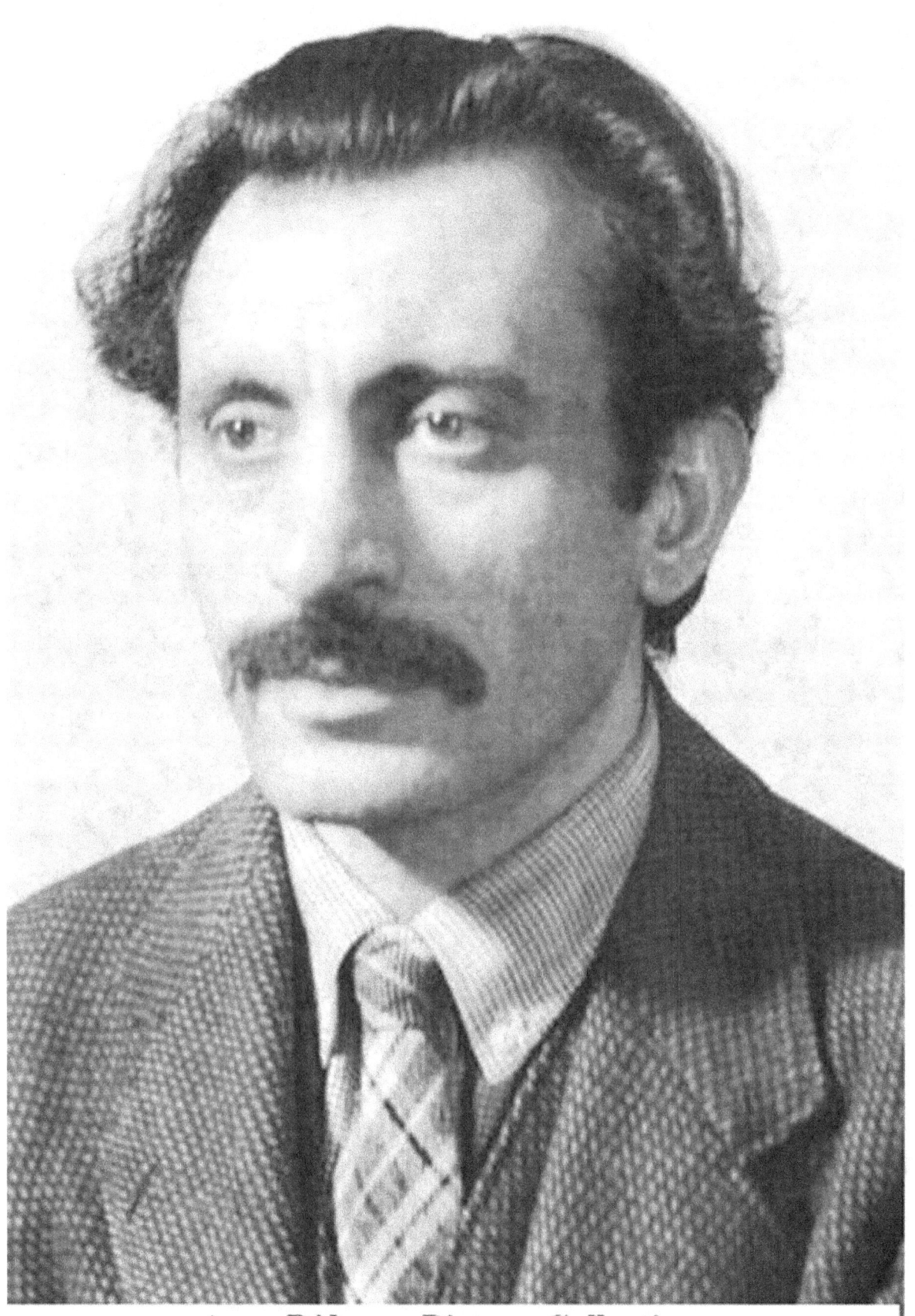

Arya Bàhram Picture Collection
ARSHILE GORKI (1904 - 1948) Armenia

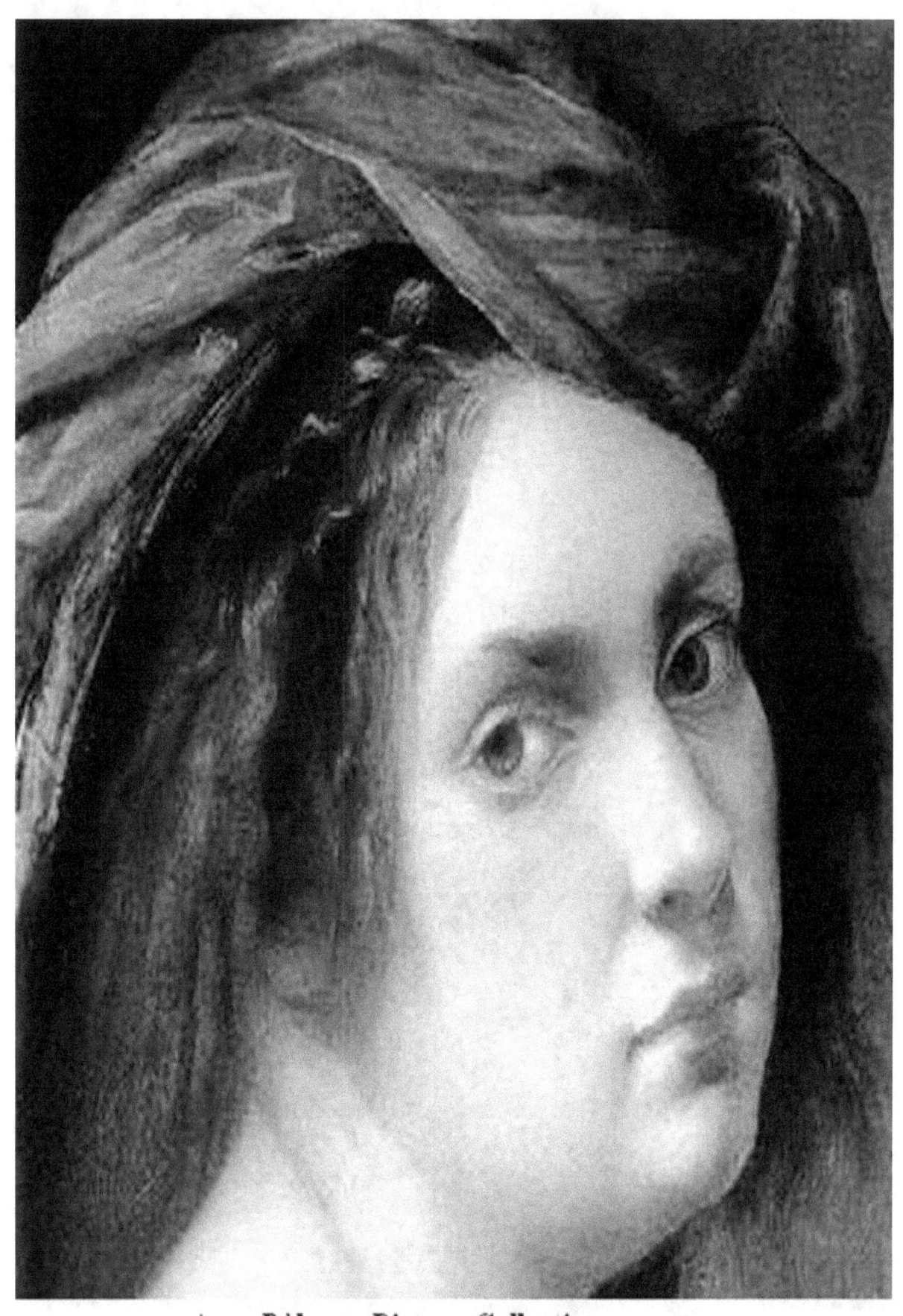

Arya Bàhram Picture Collection
ARTEMISIA GENTILESCHI (1593-1656) Italy

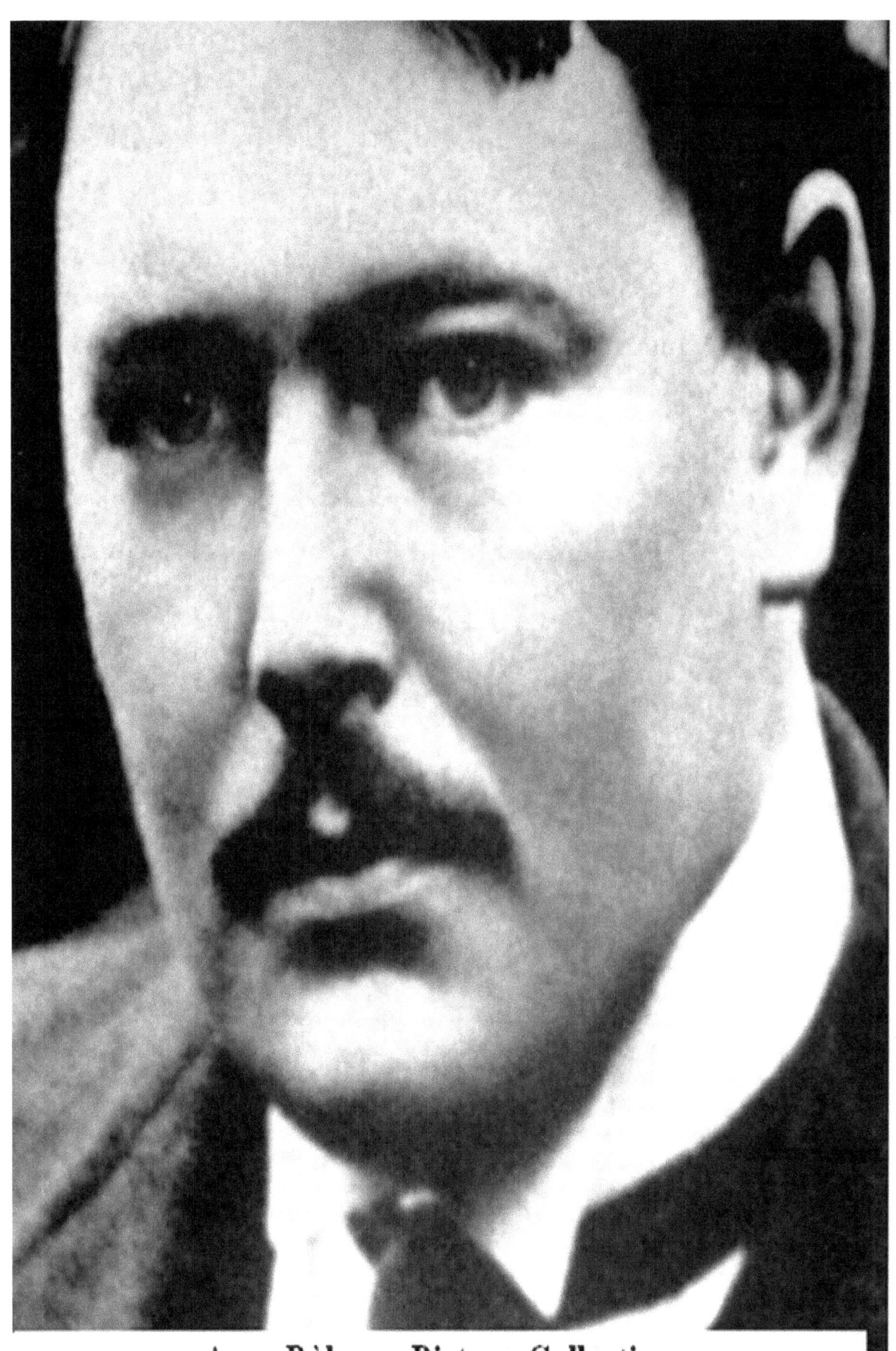

AUGUST MACKE (1887-1914) Germany

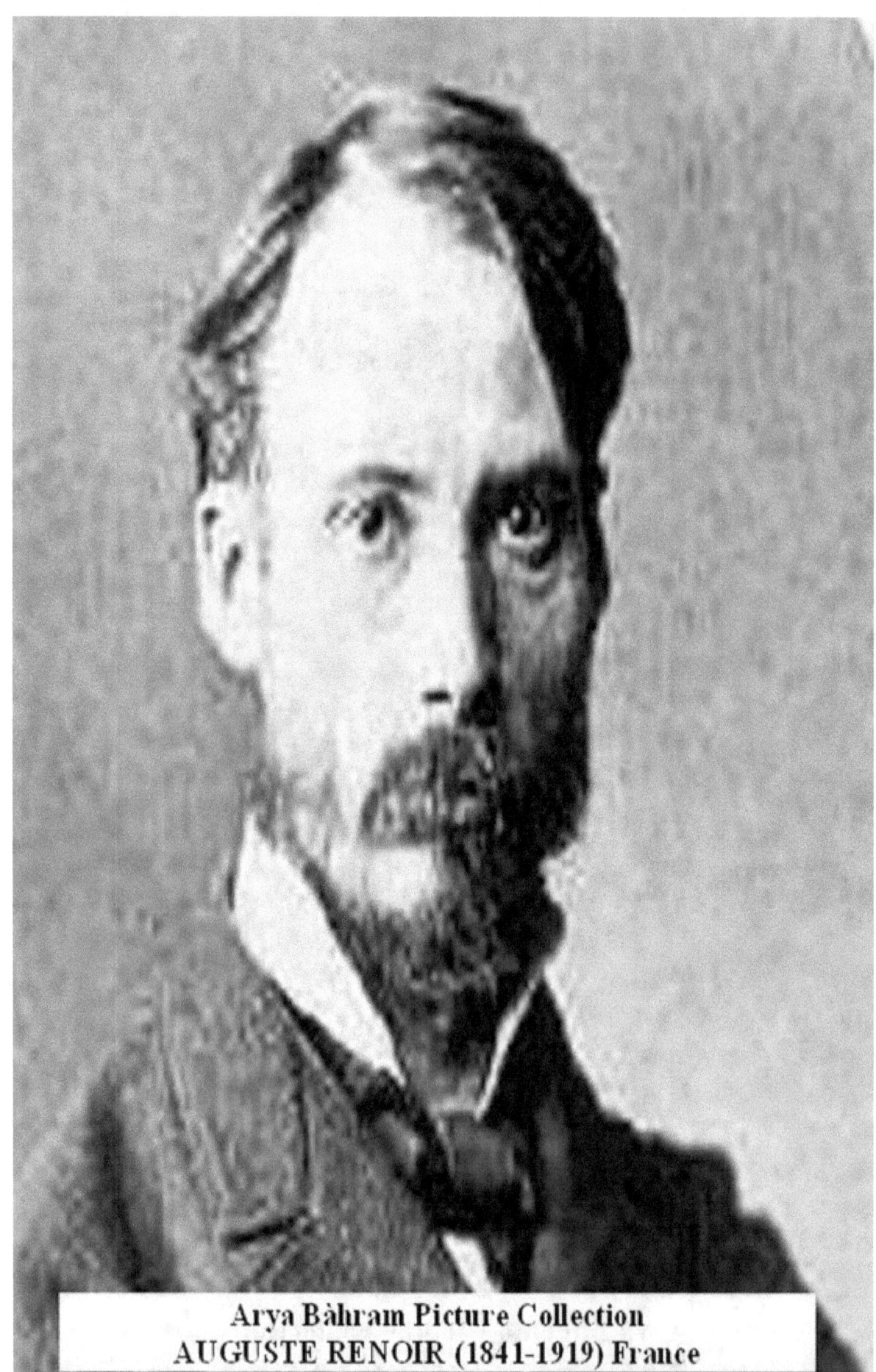

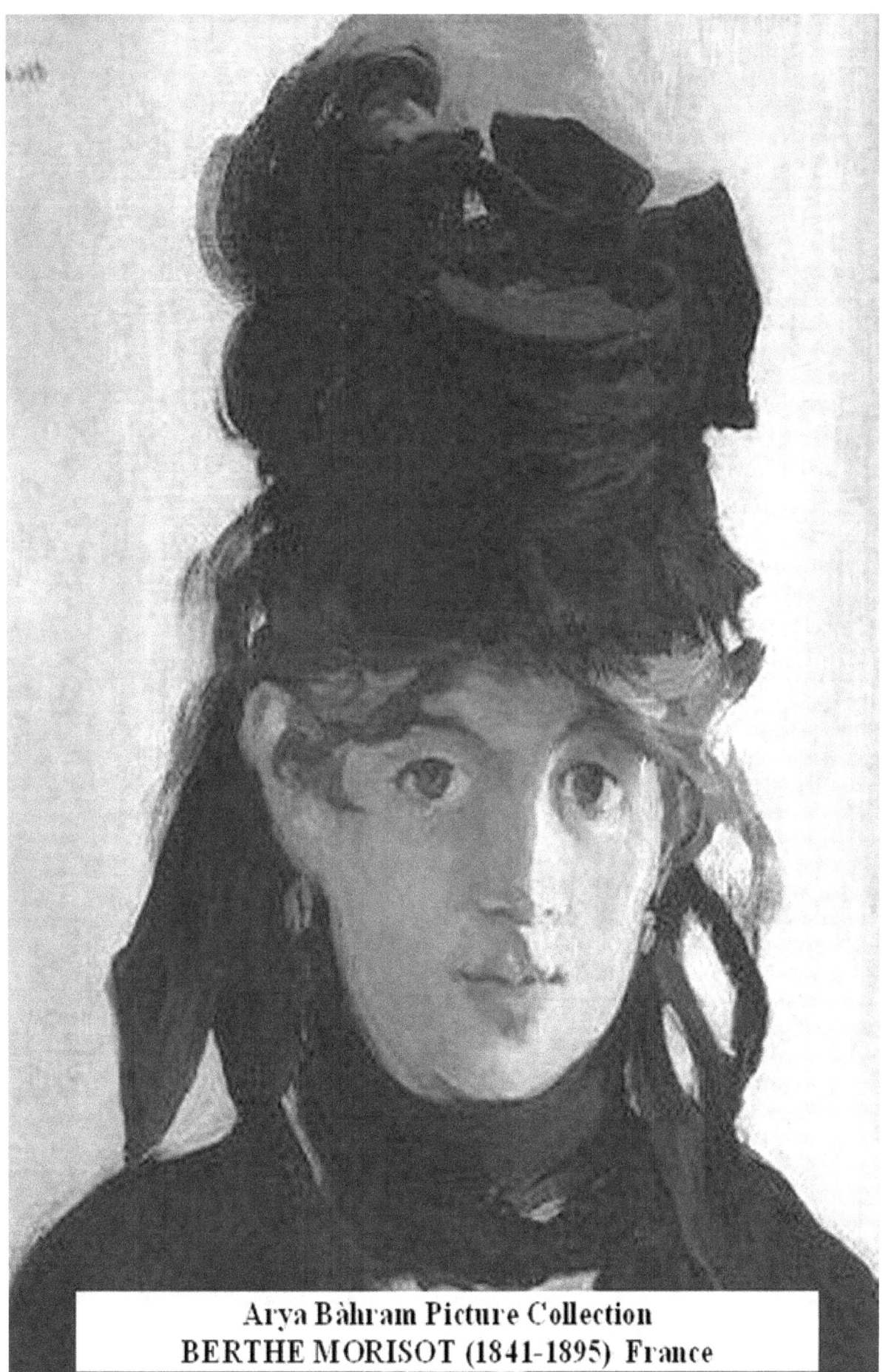

BERTHE MORISOT (1841-1895) France

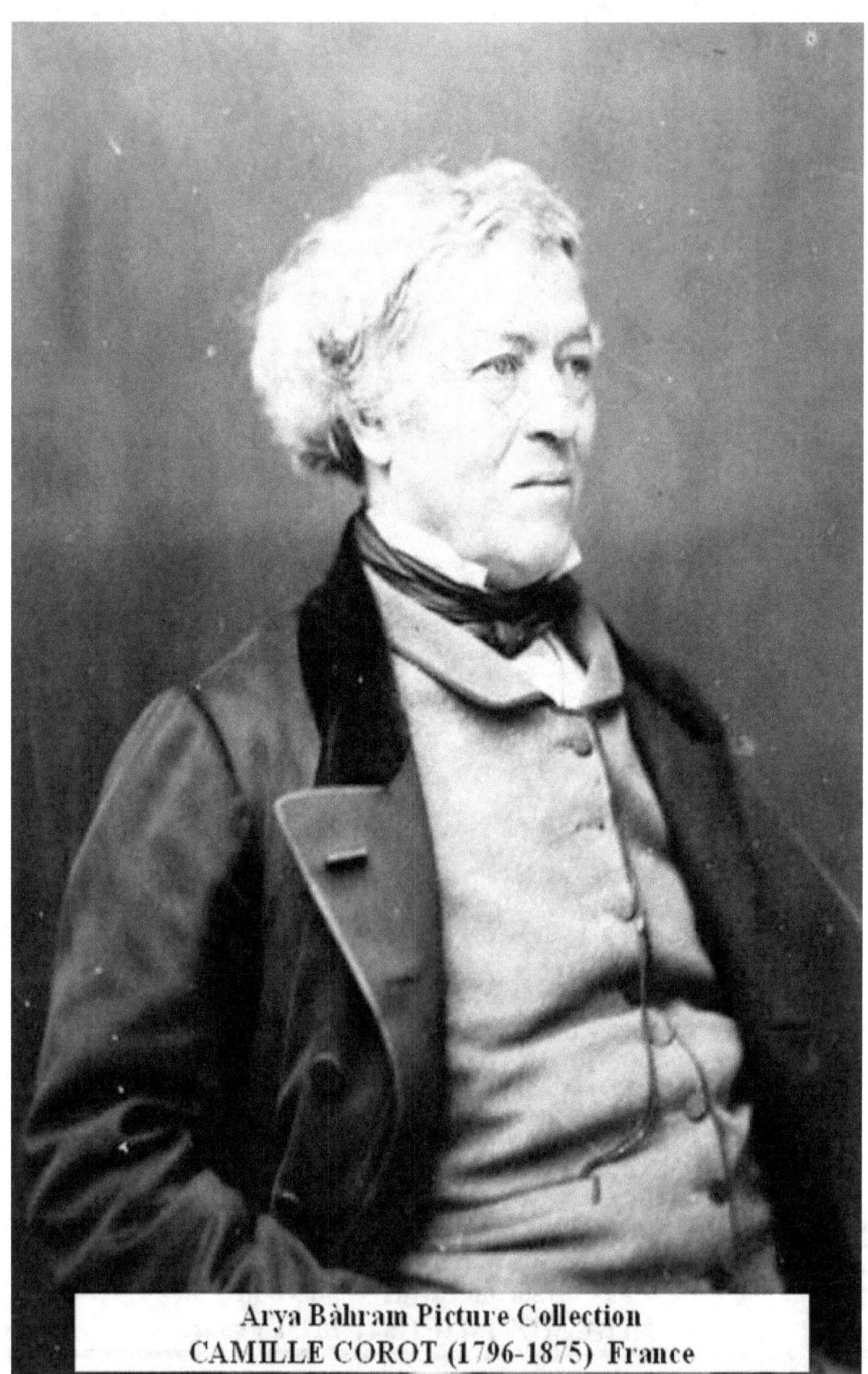

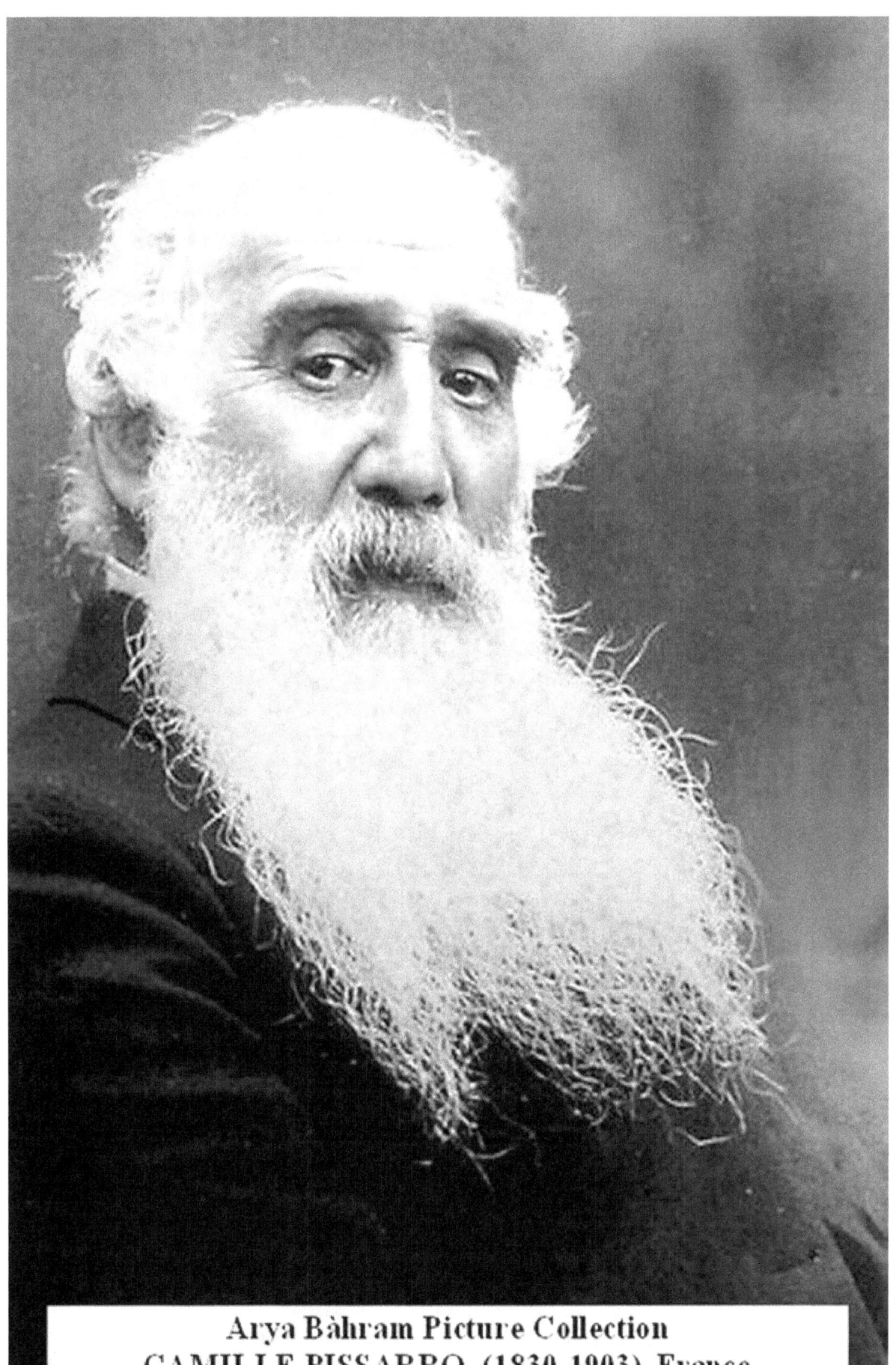

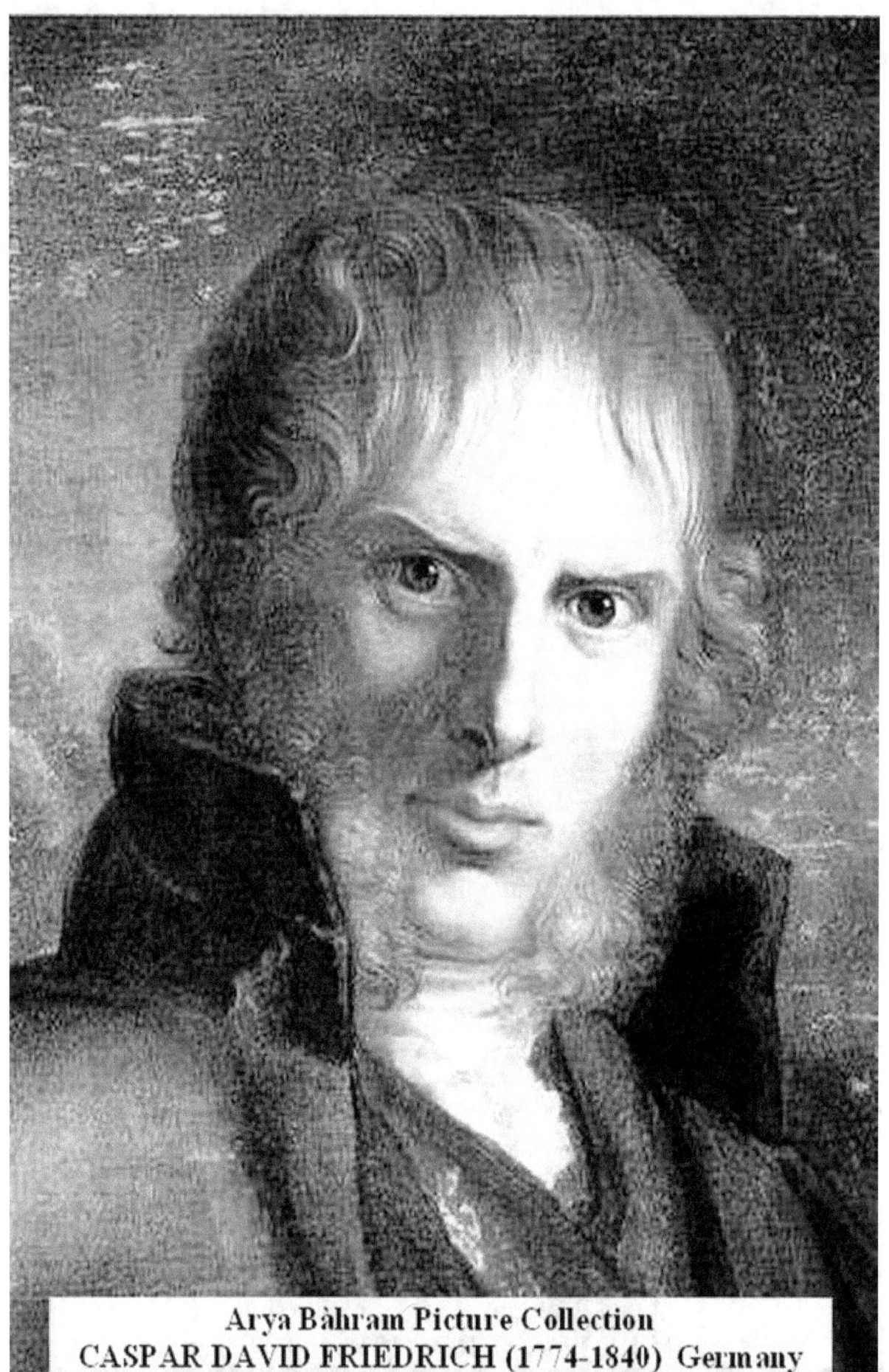

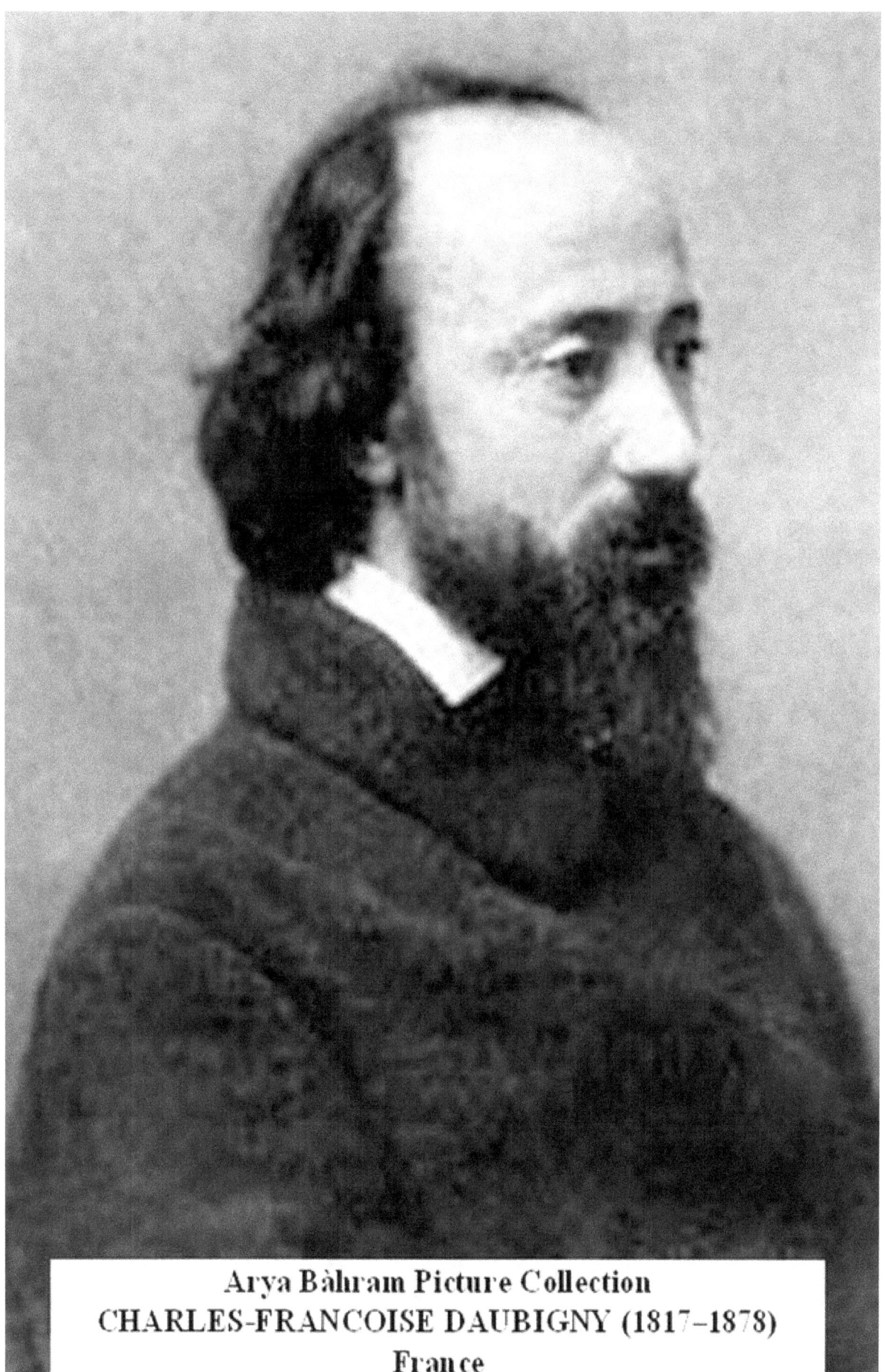

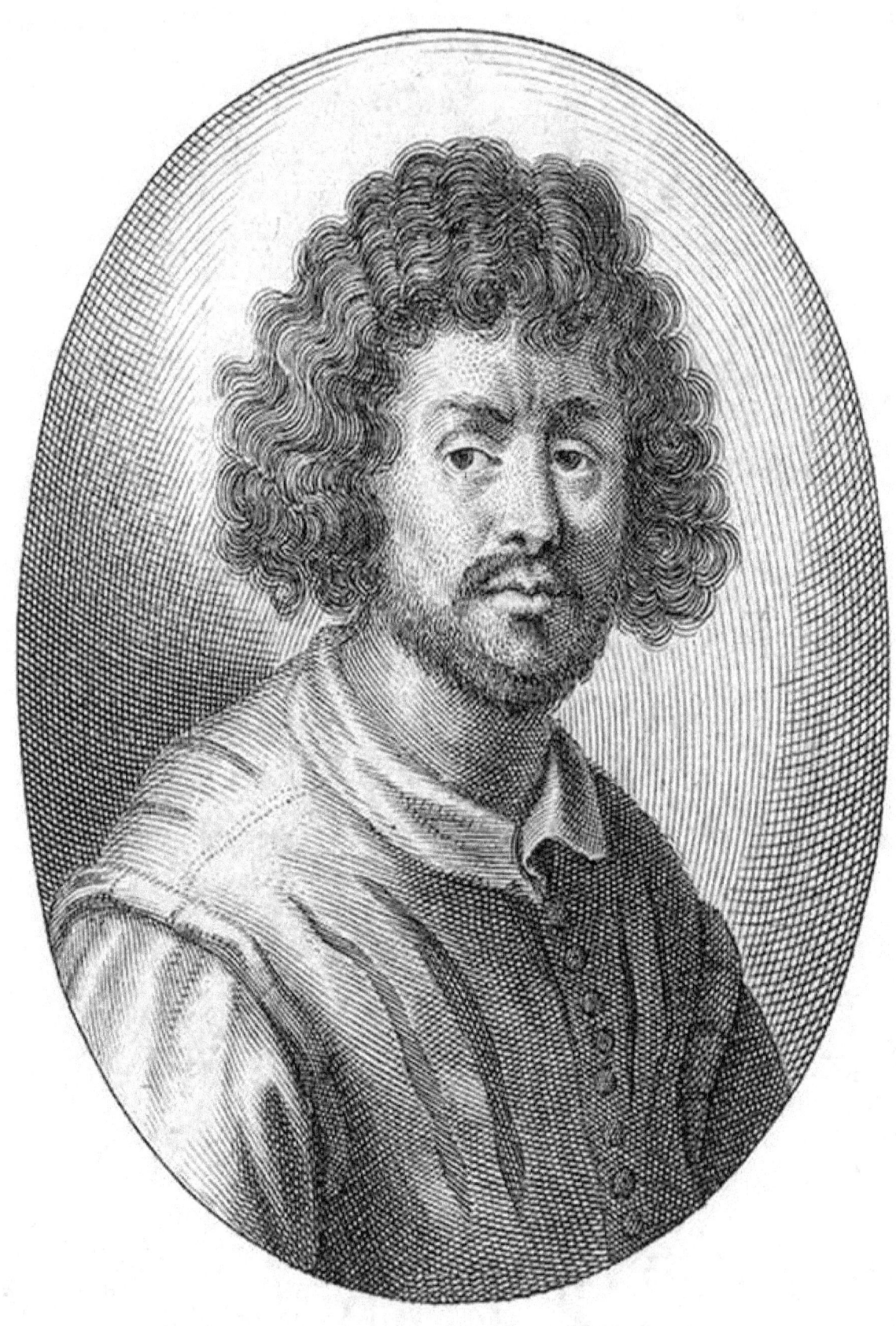

CLAUDE LORRAIN (1600-1682) France

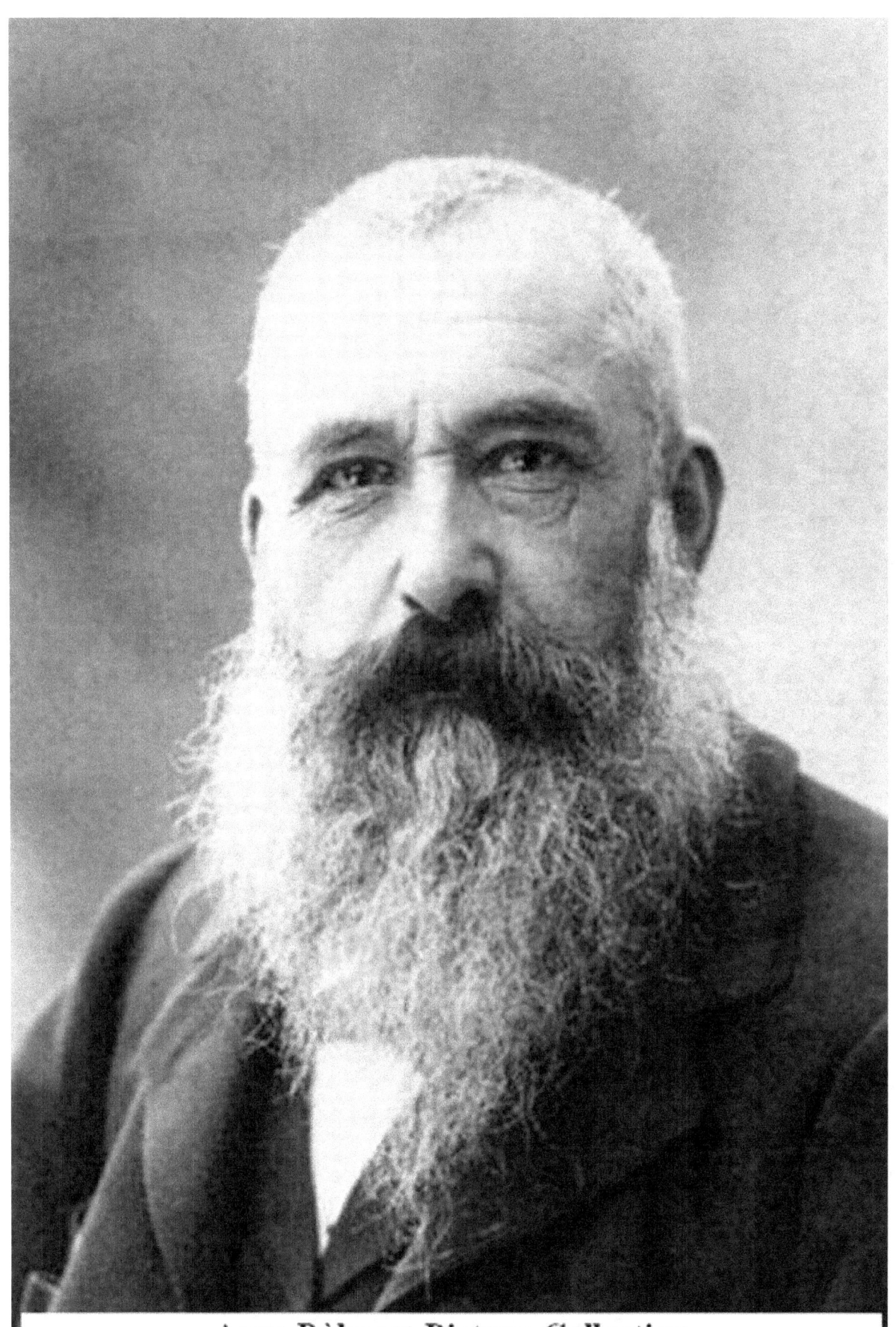

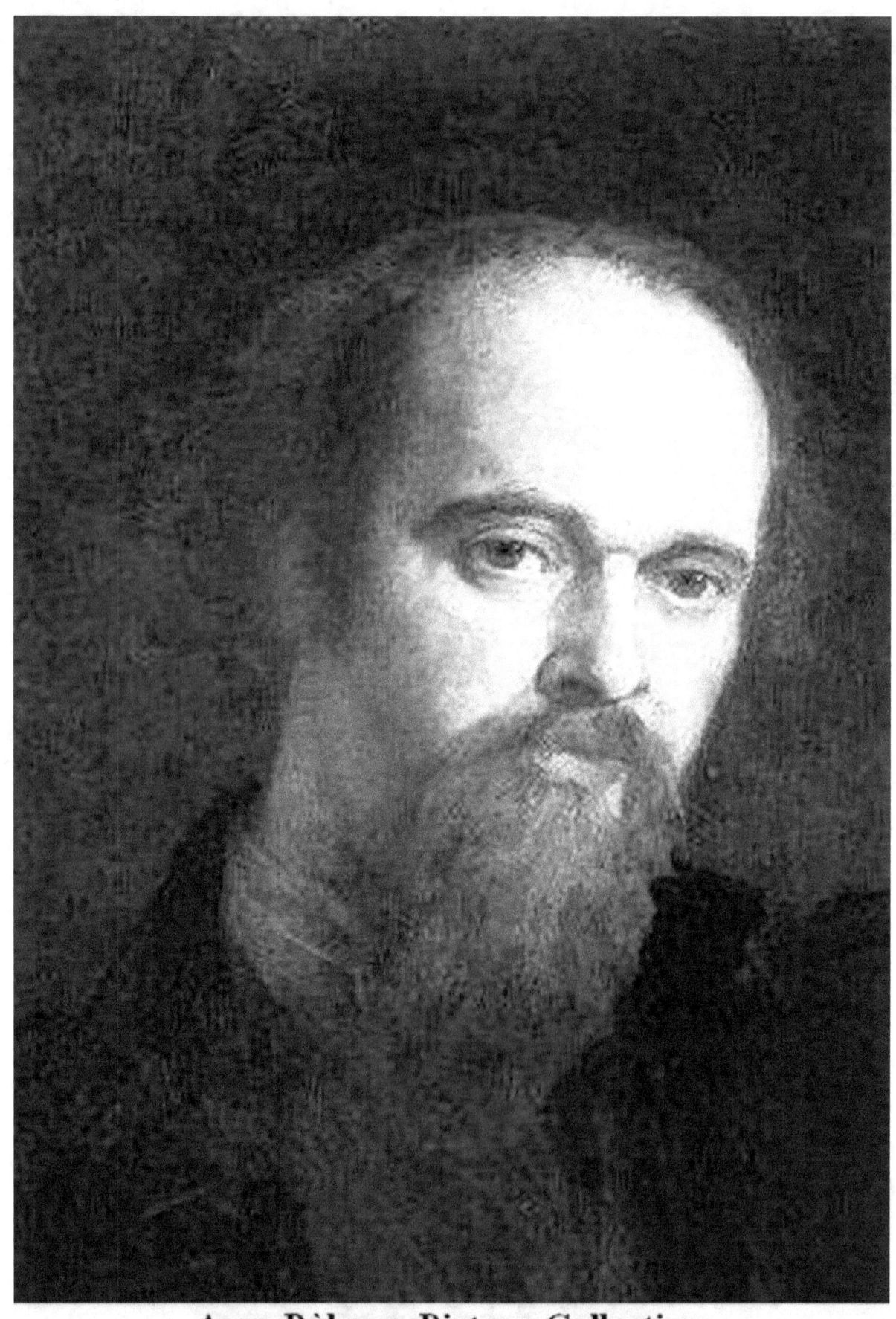

Arya Bàhram Picture Collection
DANTE GABRIEL ROSSETTI (1828–1882) England

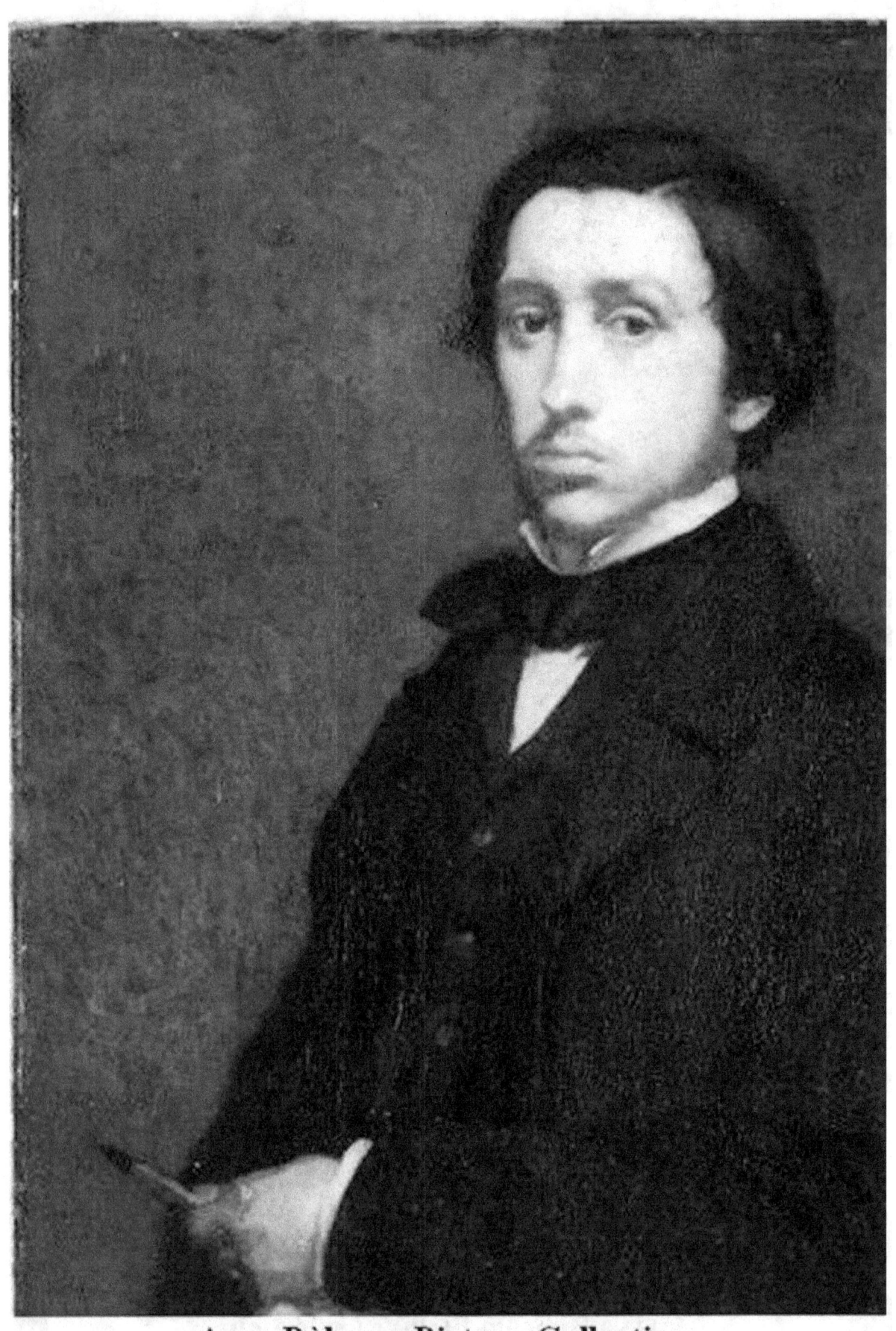

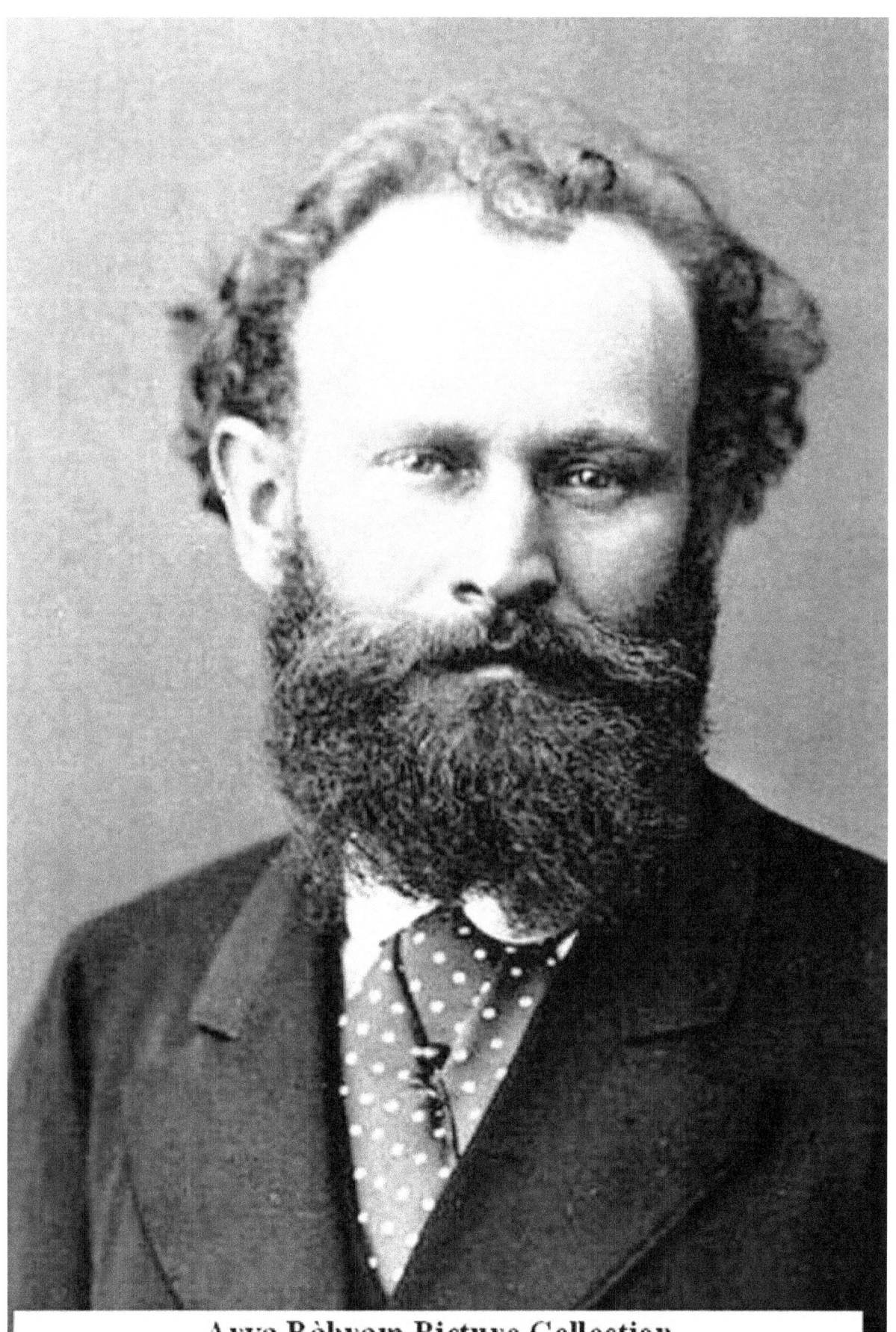

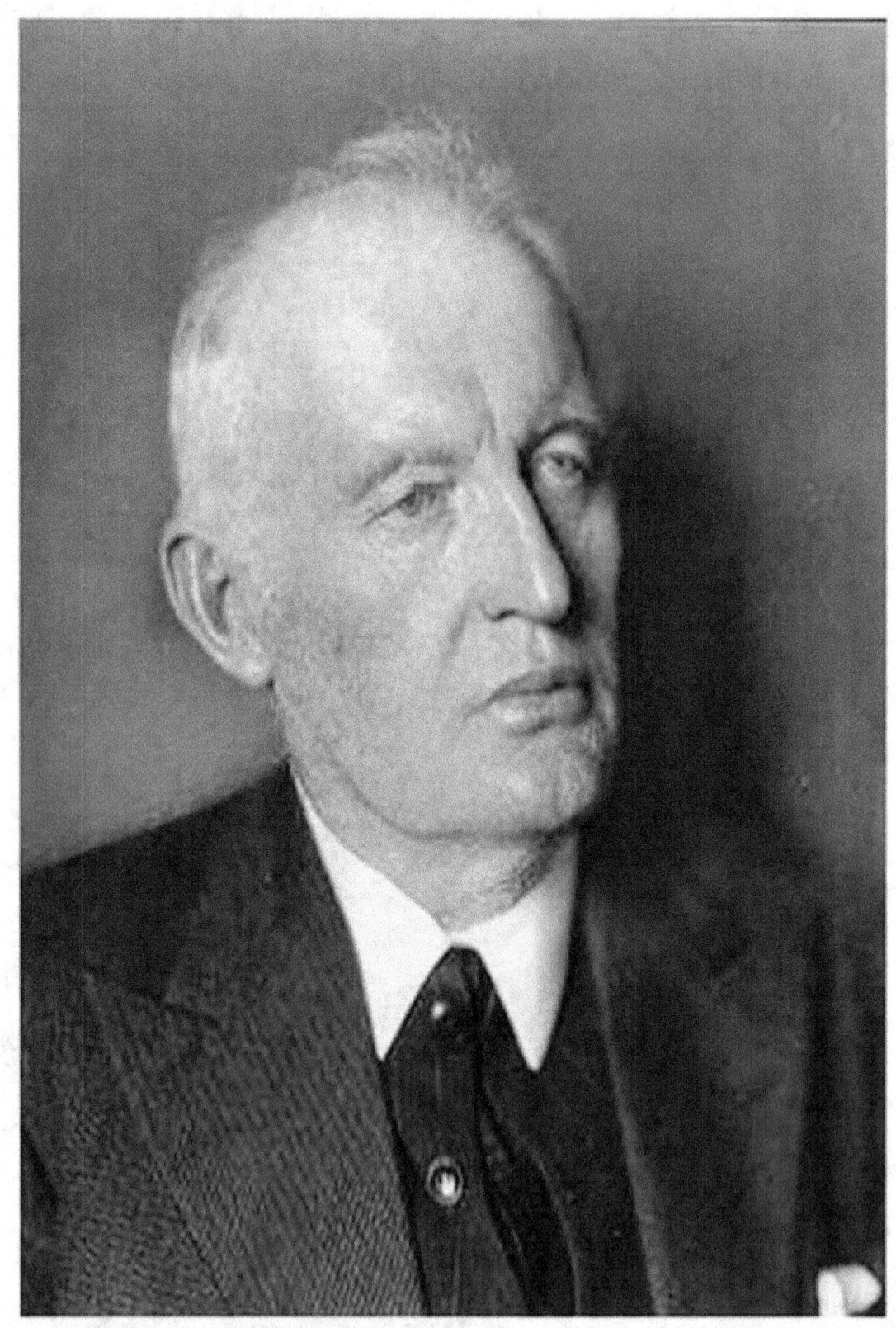

Arya Bàhram Picture Collection
EDVARD MUNCH (1863-1944) Norway

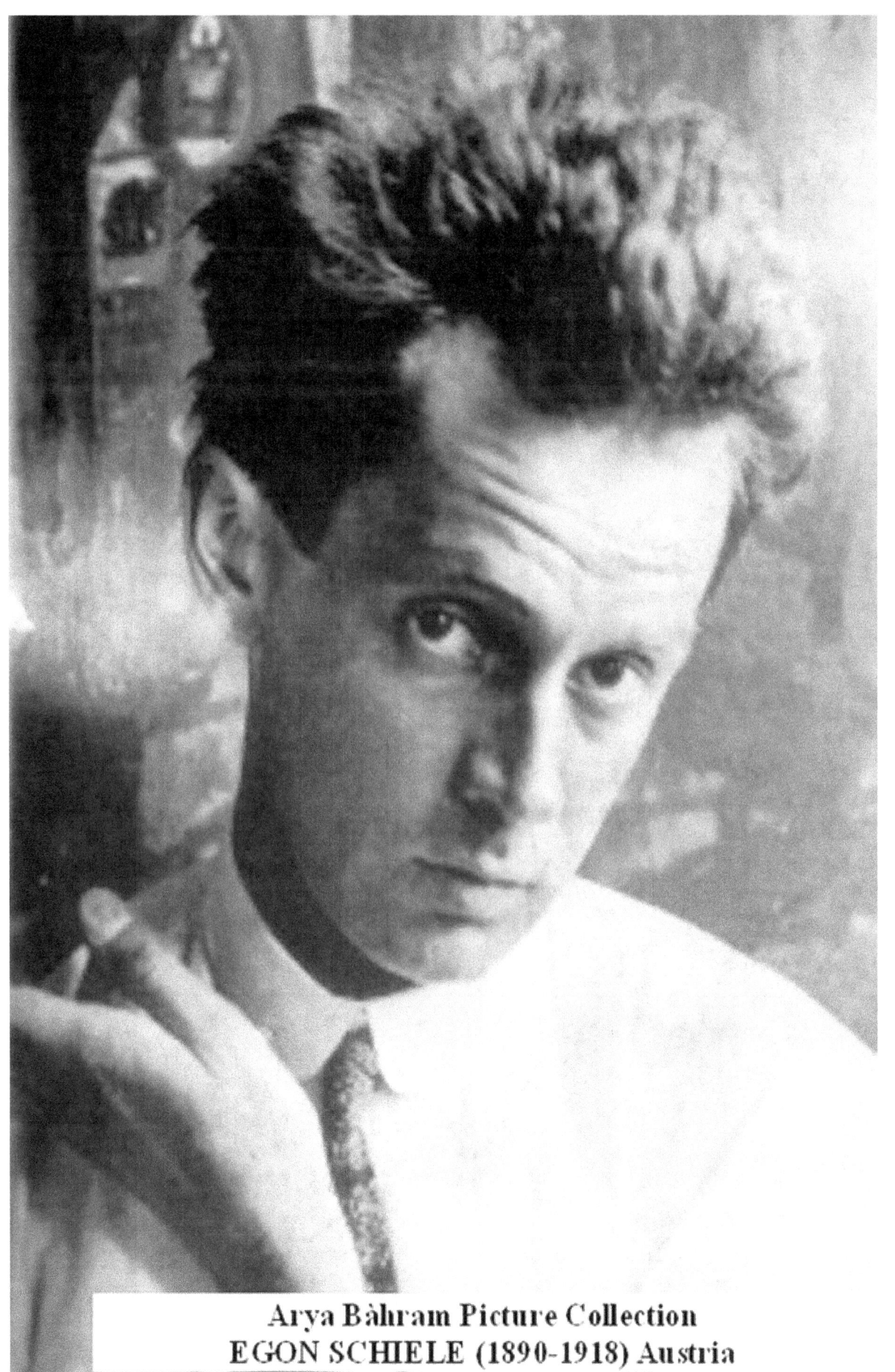

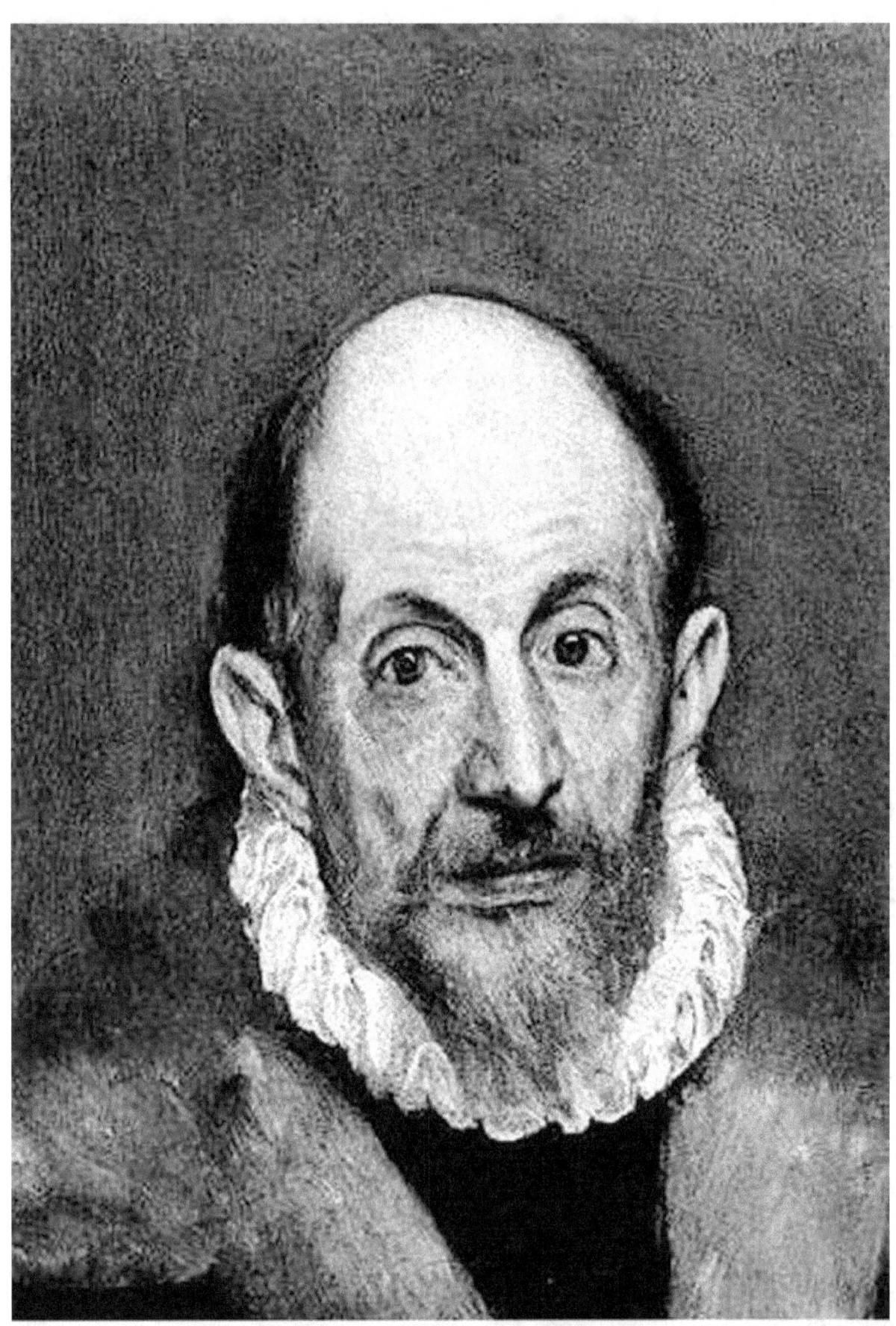

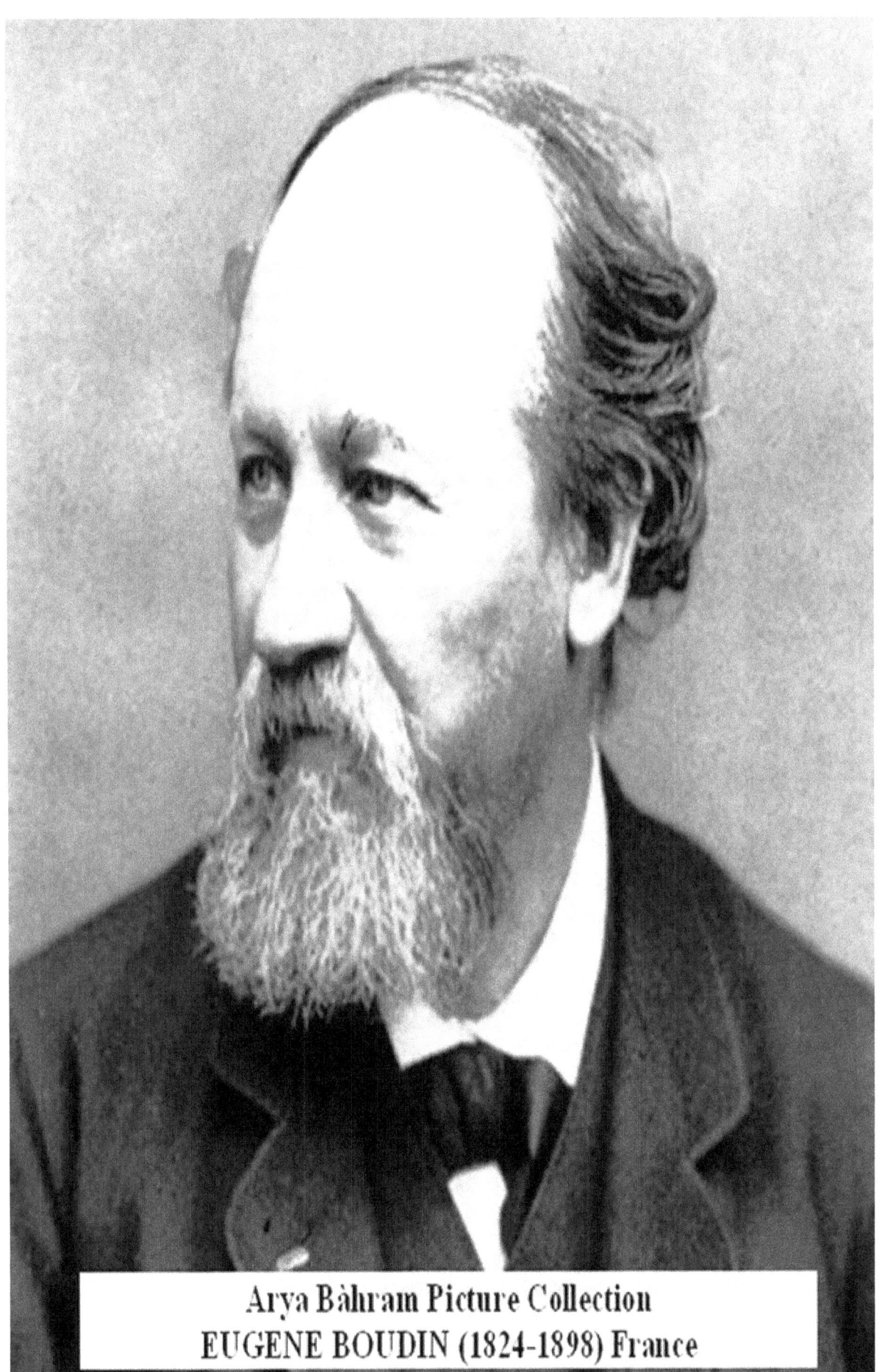

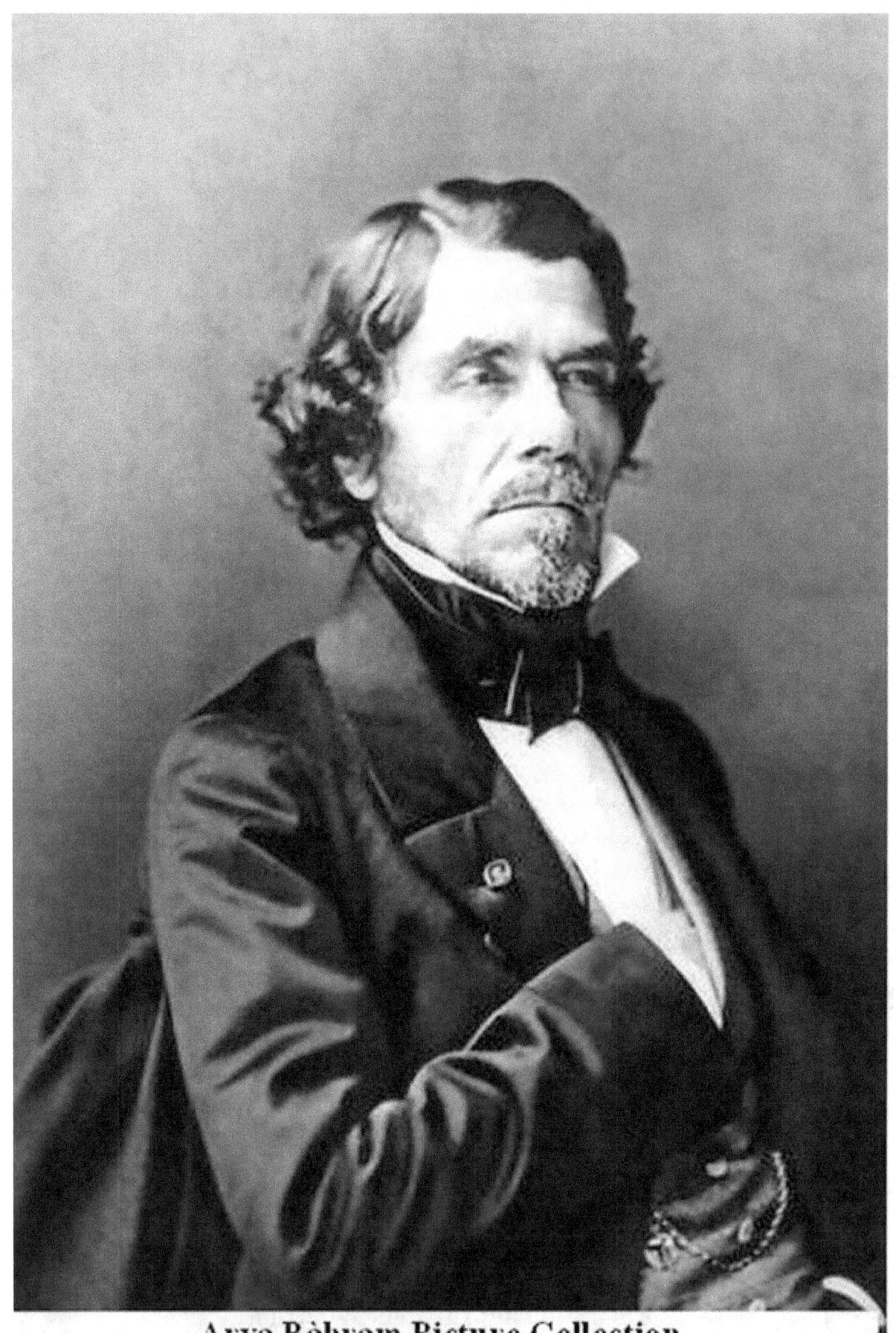

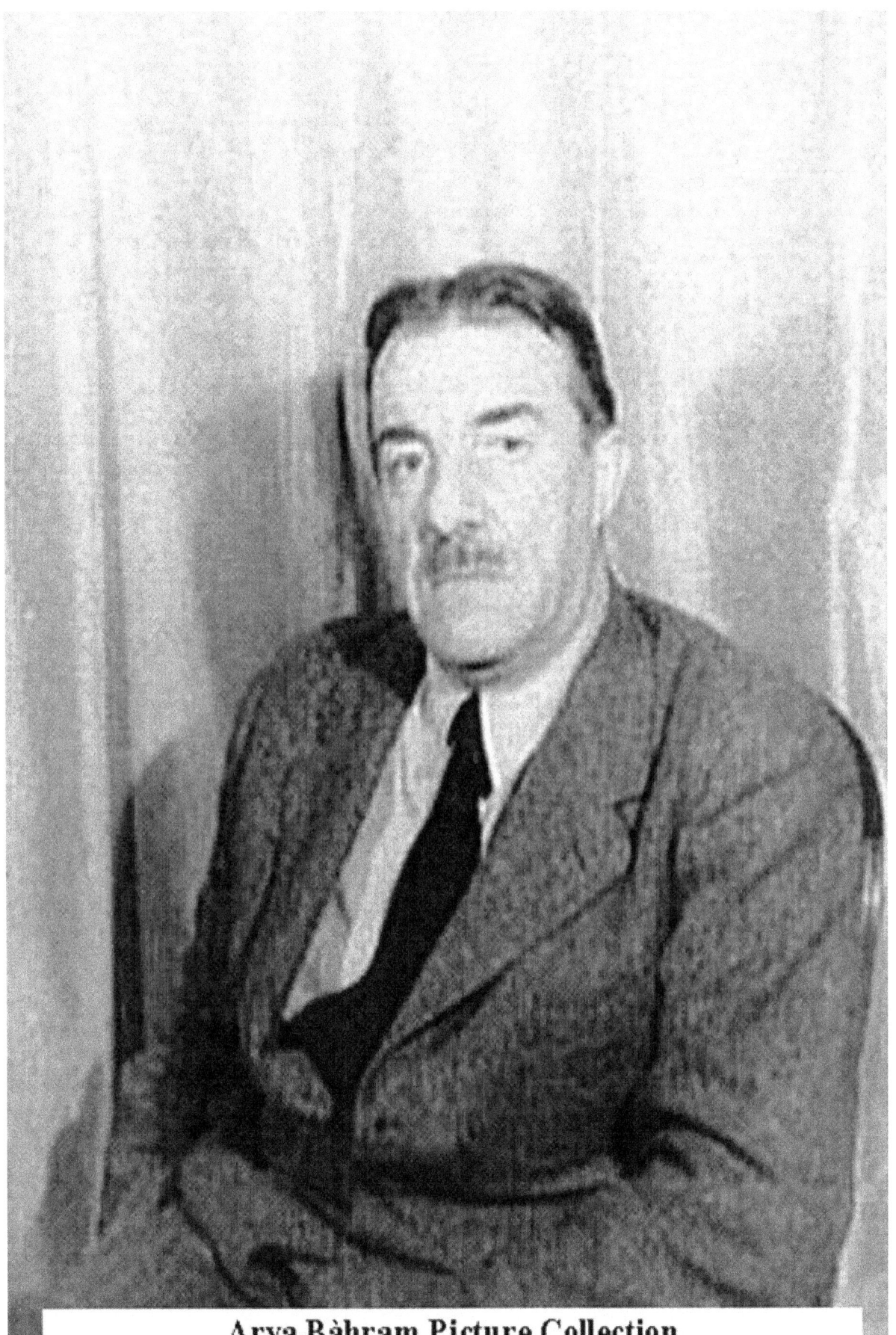

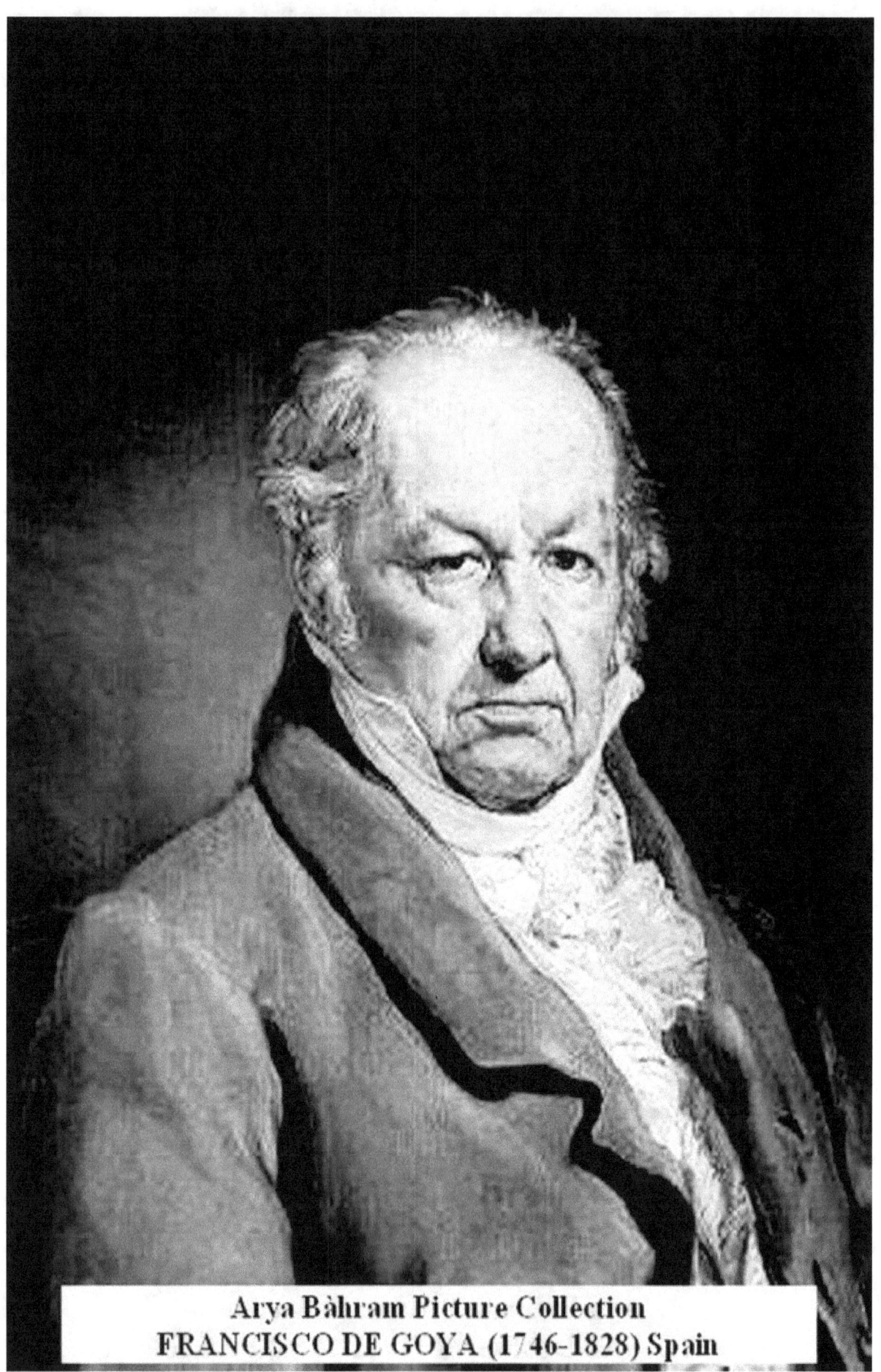

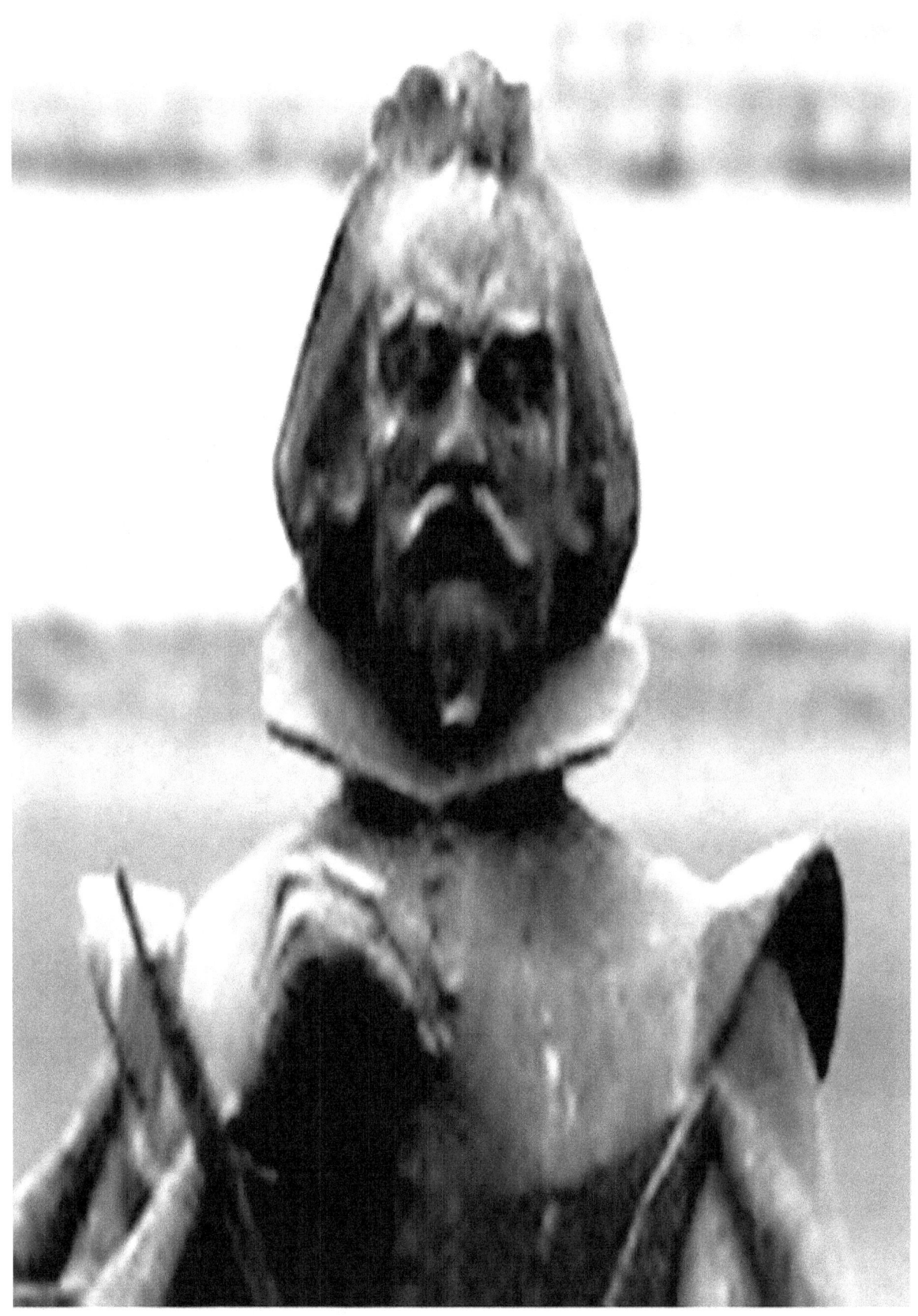

FRANCISCO DE ZURBARÁN (1598-1664) Spain

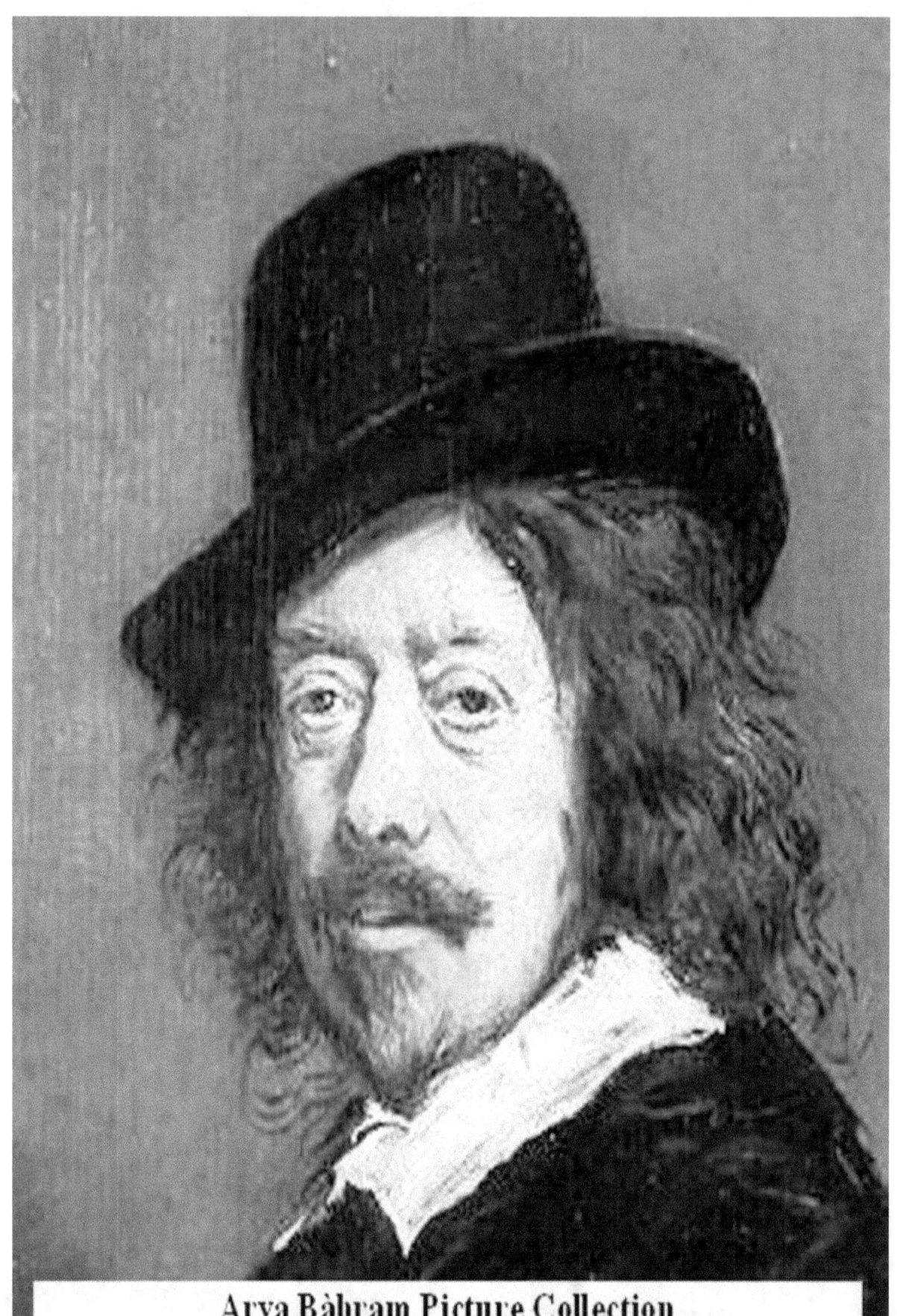

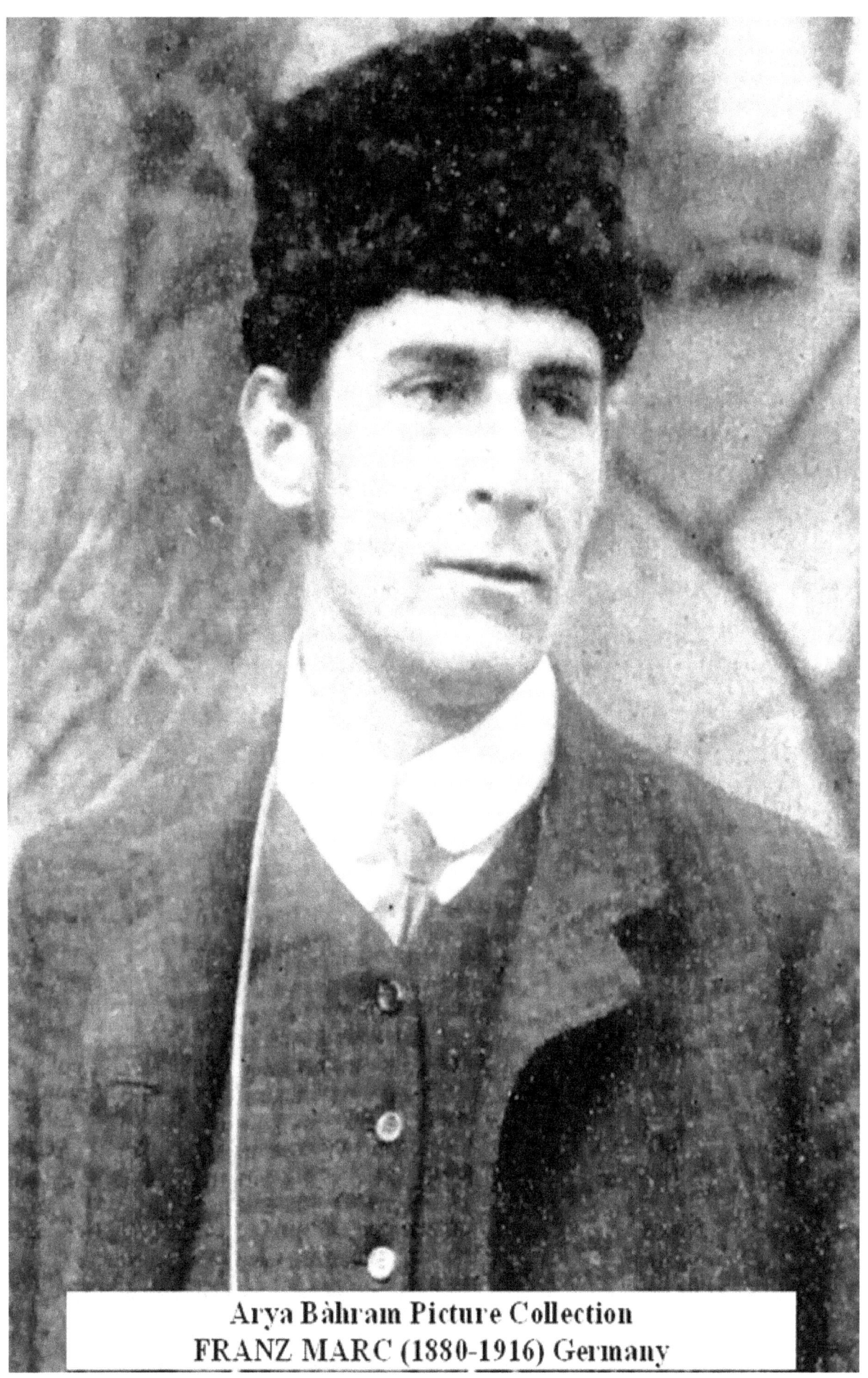

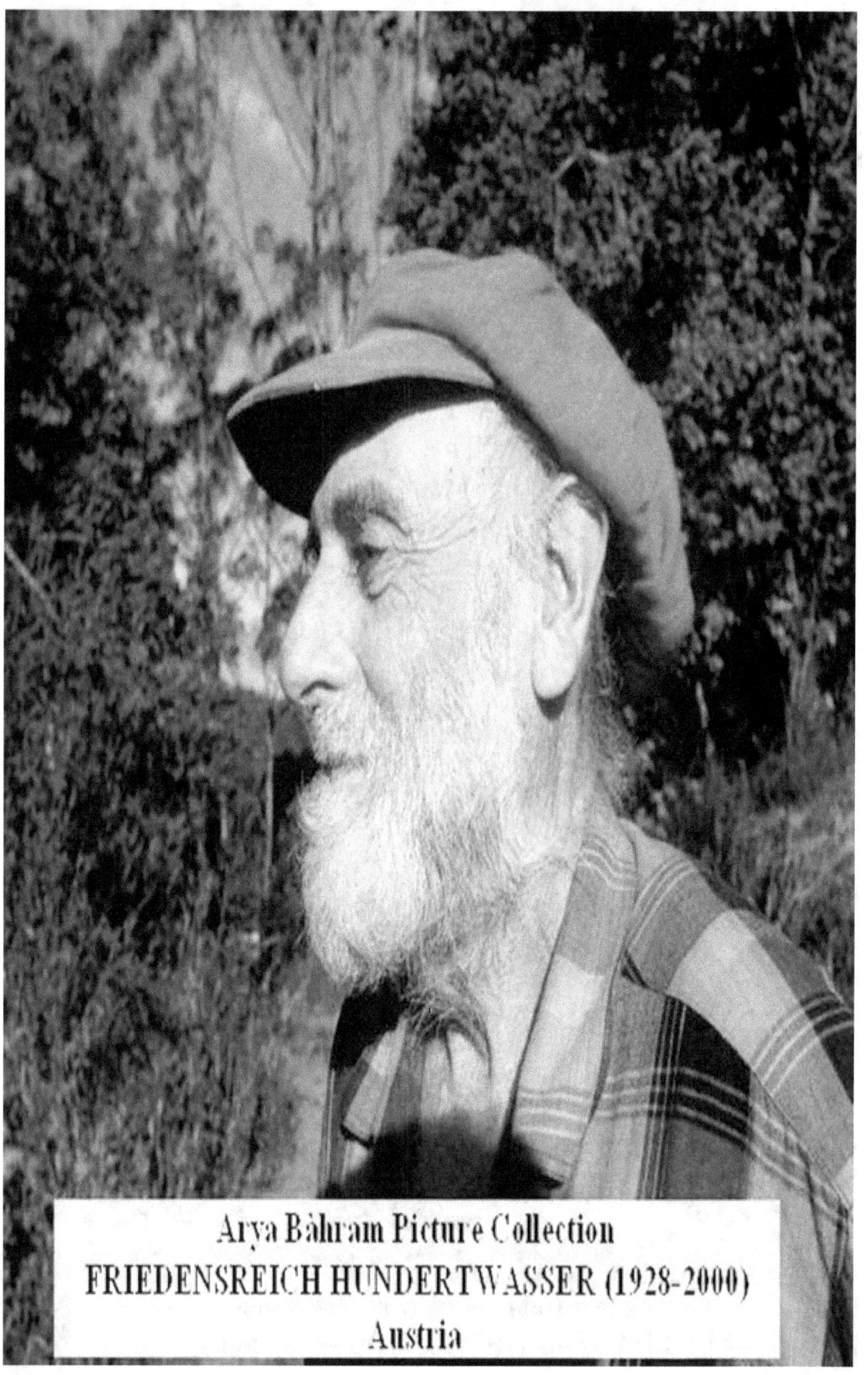

Arya Bahram Picture Collection
FRIEDENSREICH HUNDERTWASSER (1928-2000)
Austria

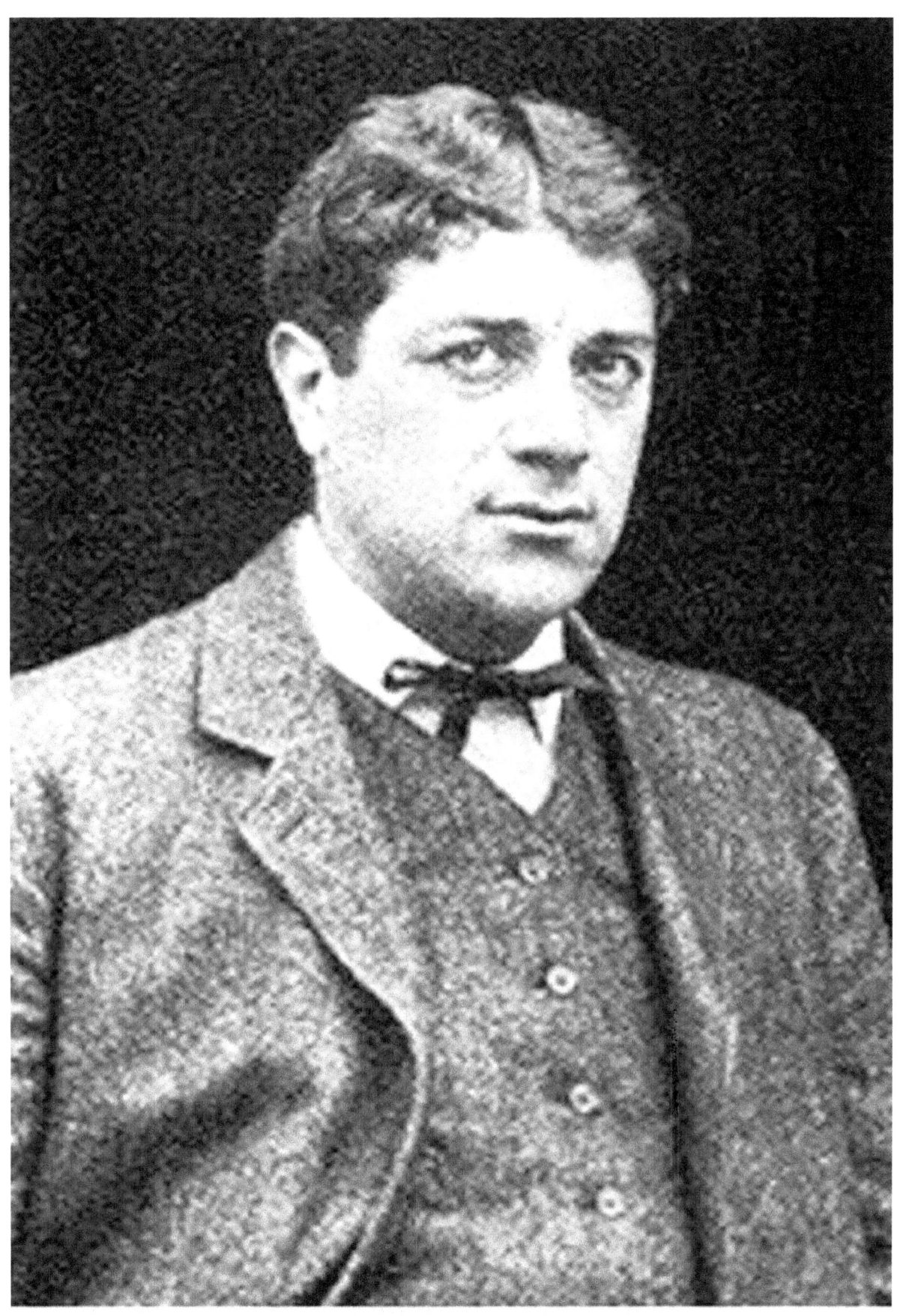

GEORGES BRAQUE (1882-1963) France

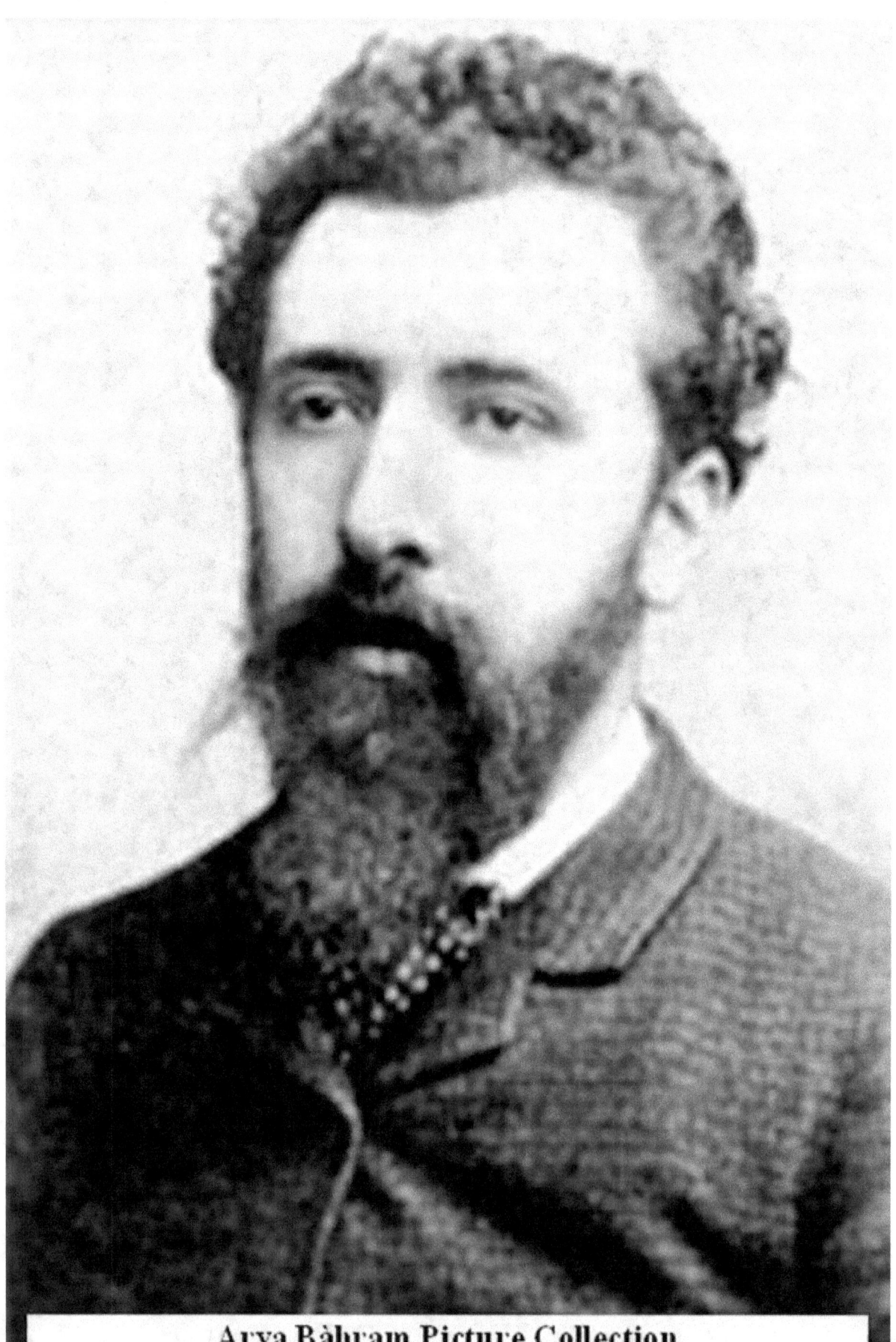

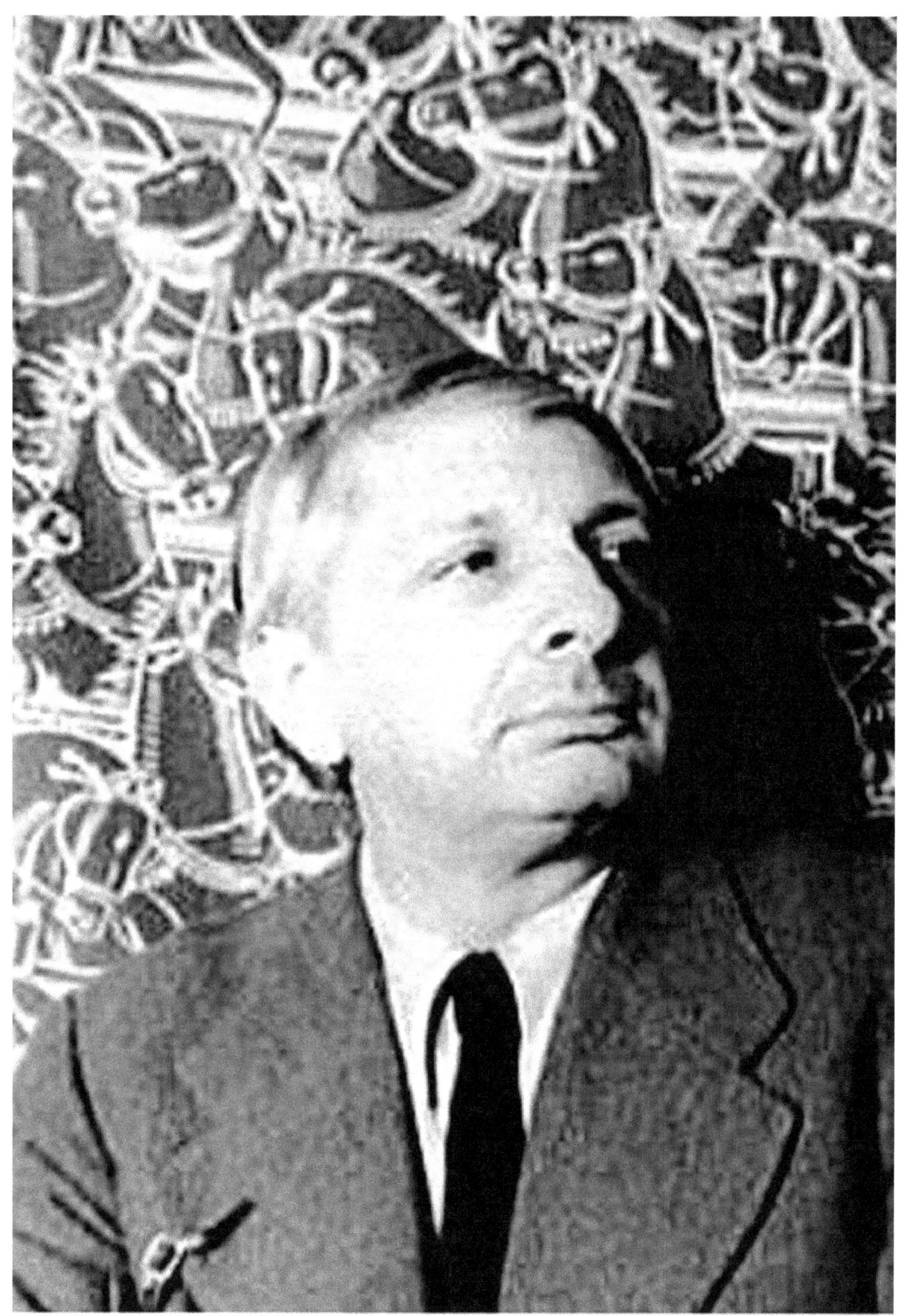

GIORGIO DE CHIRICO (1888-1978) Italy

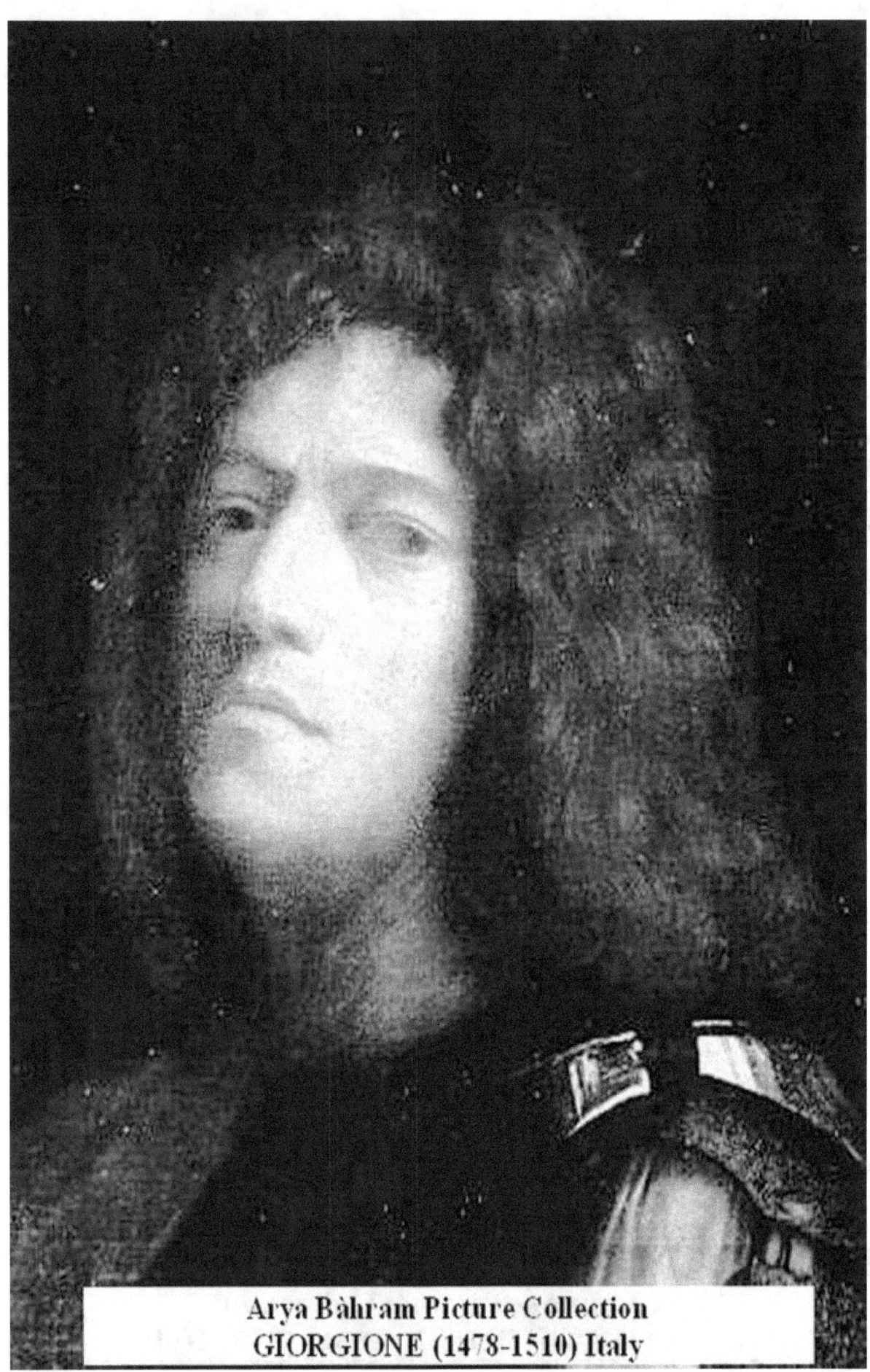

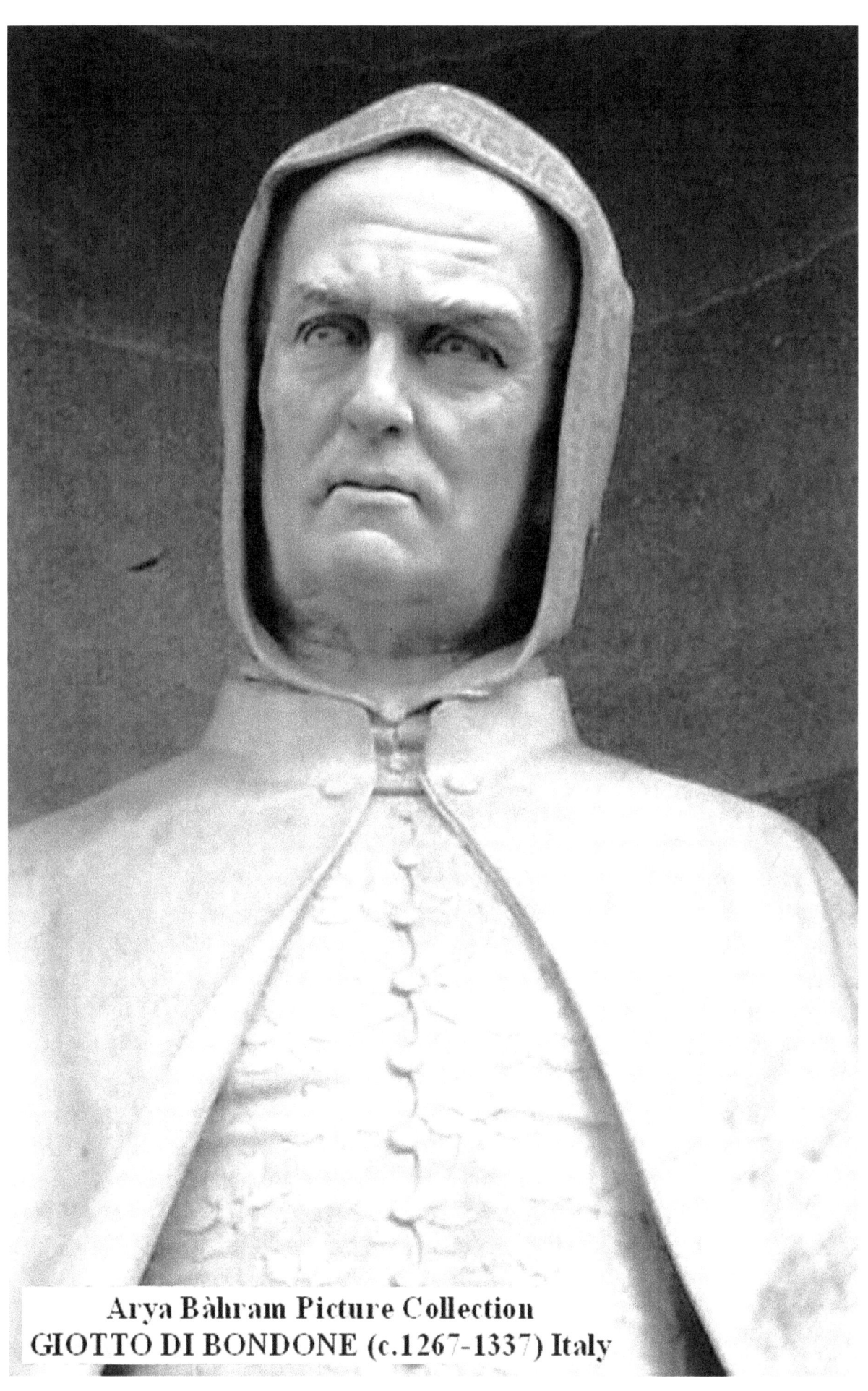

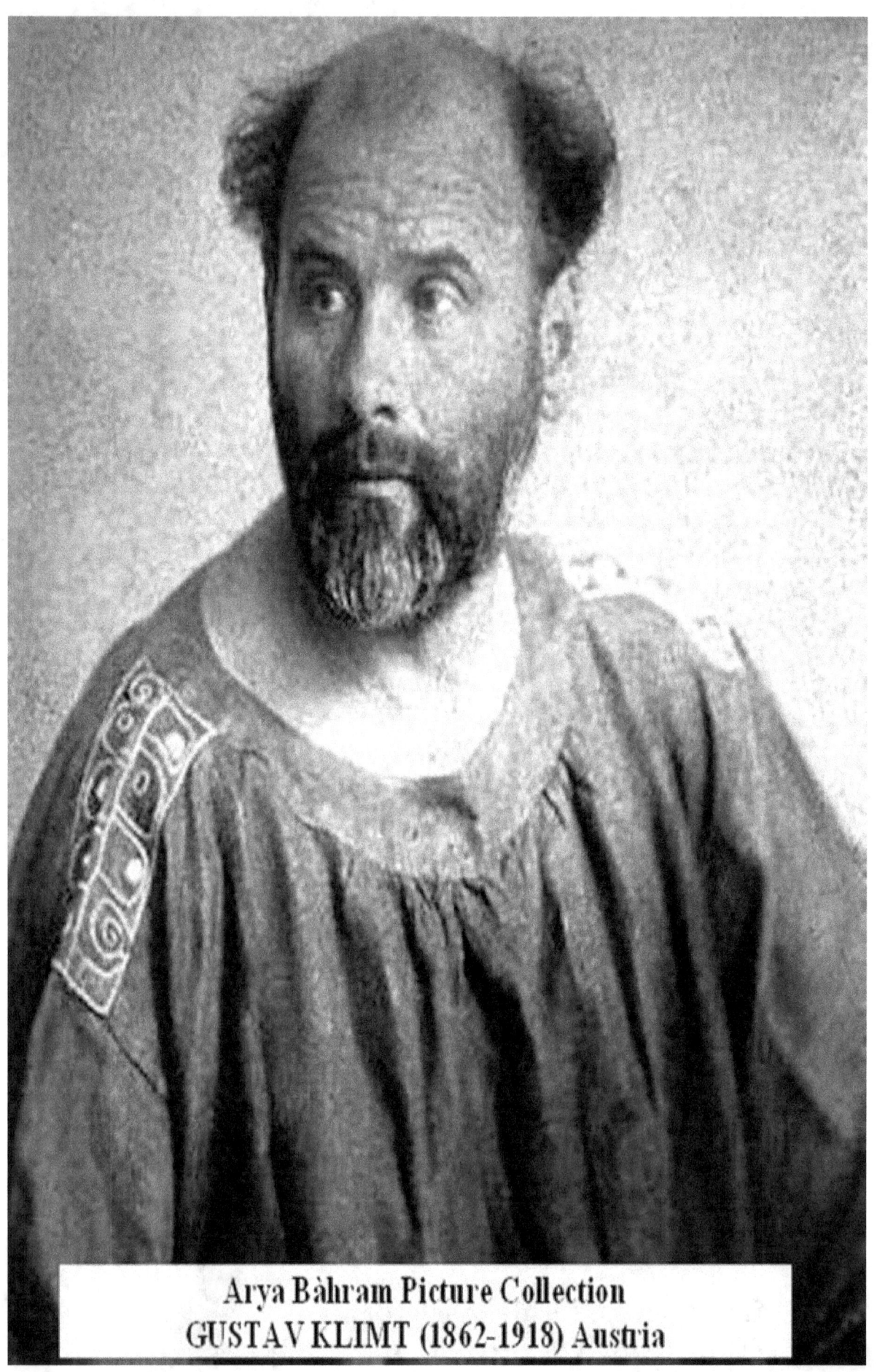

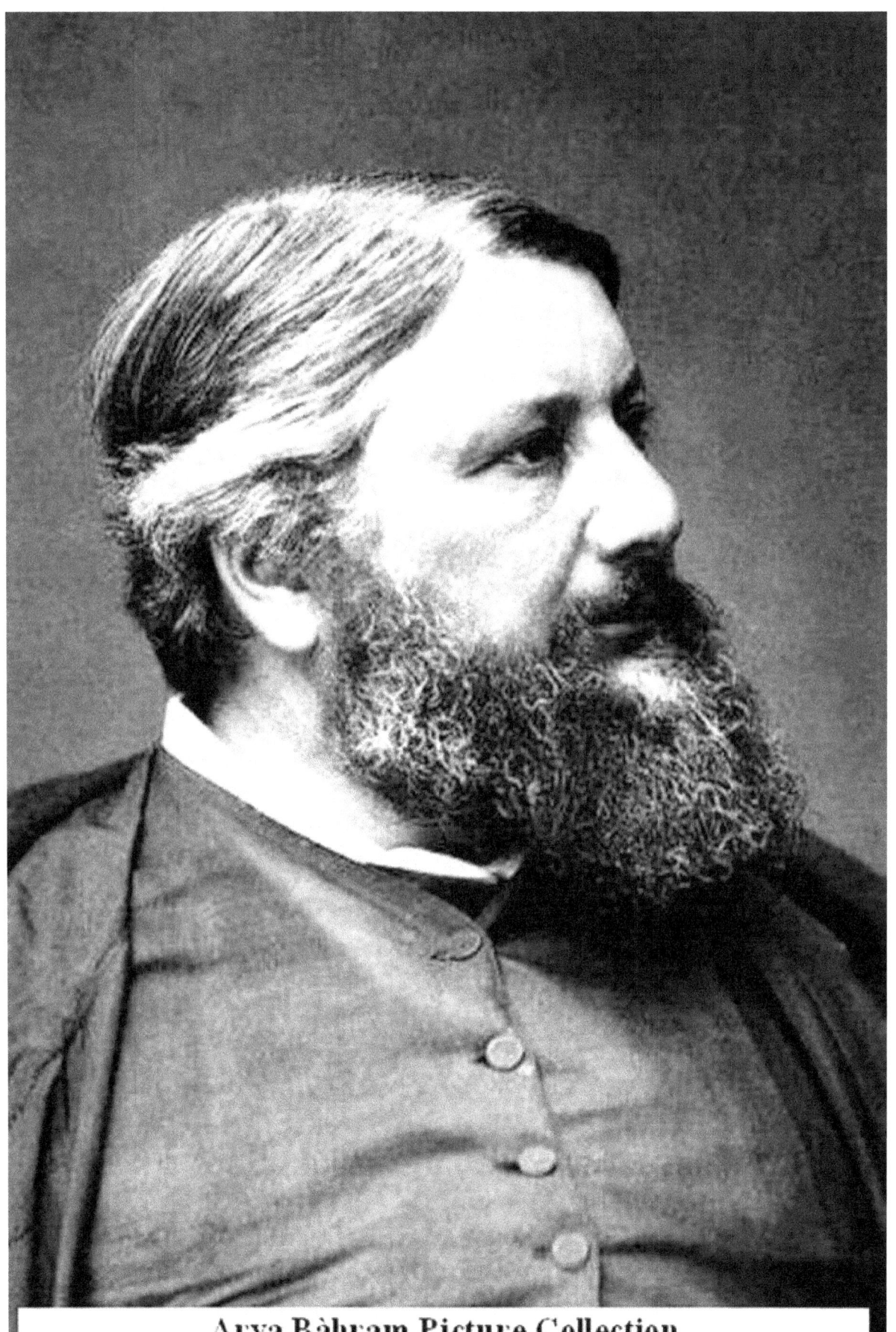

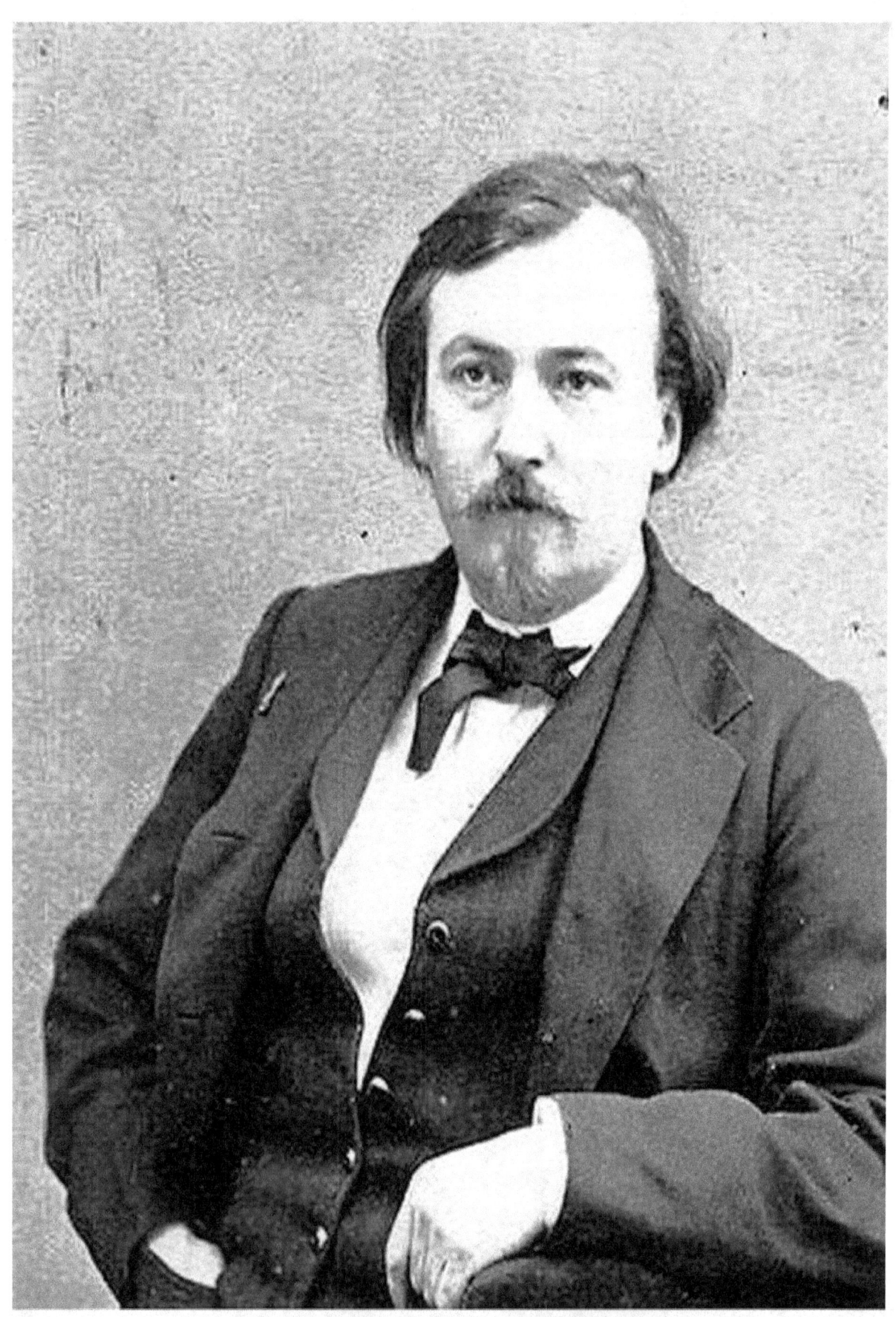

GUSTAVE DORE (1832-1883) France

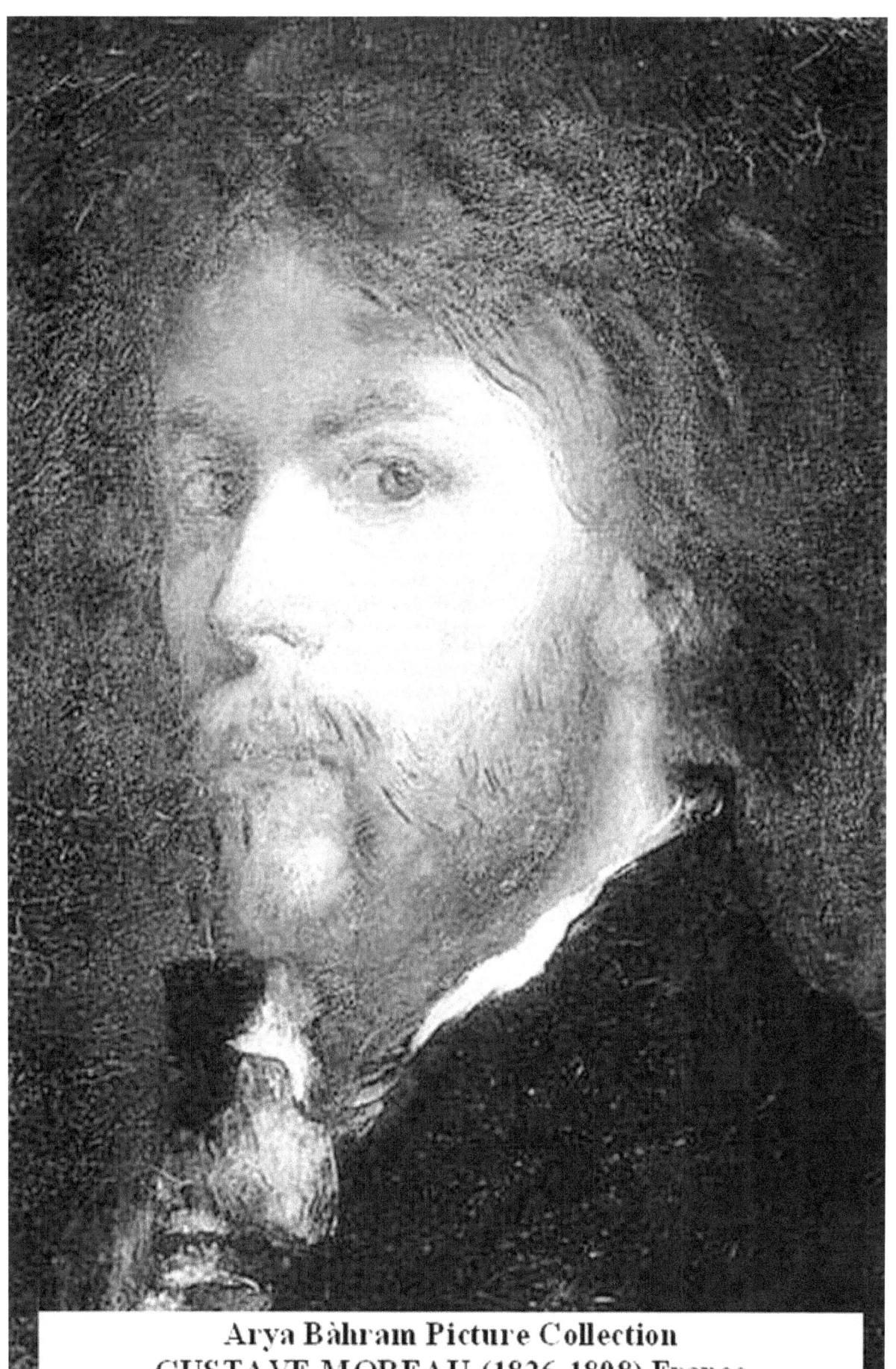

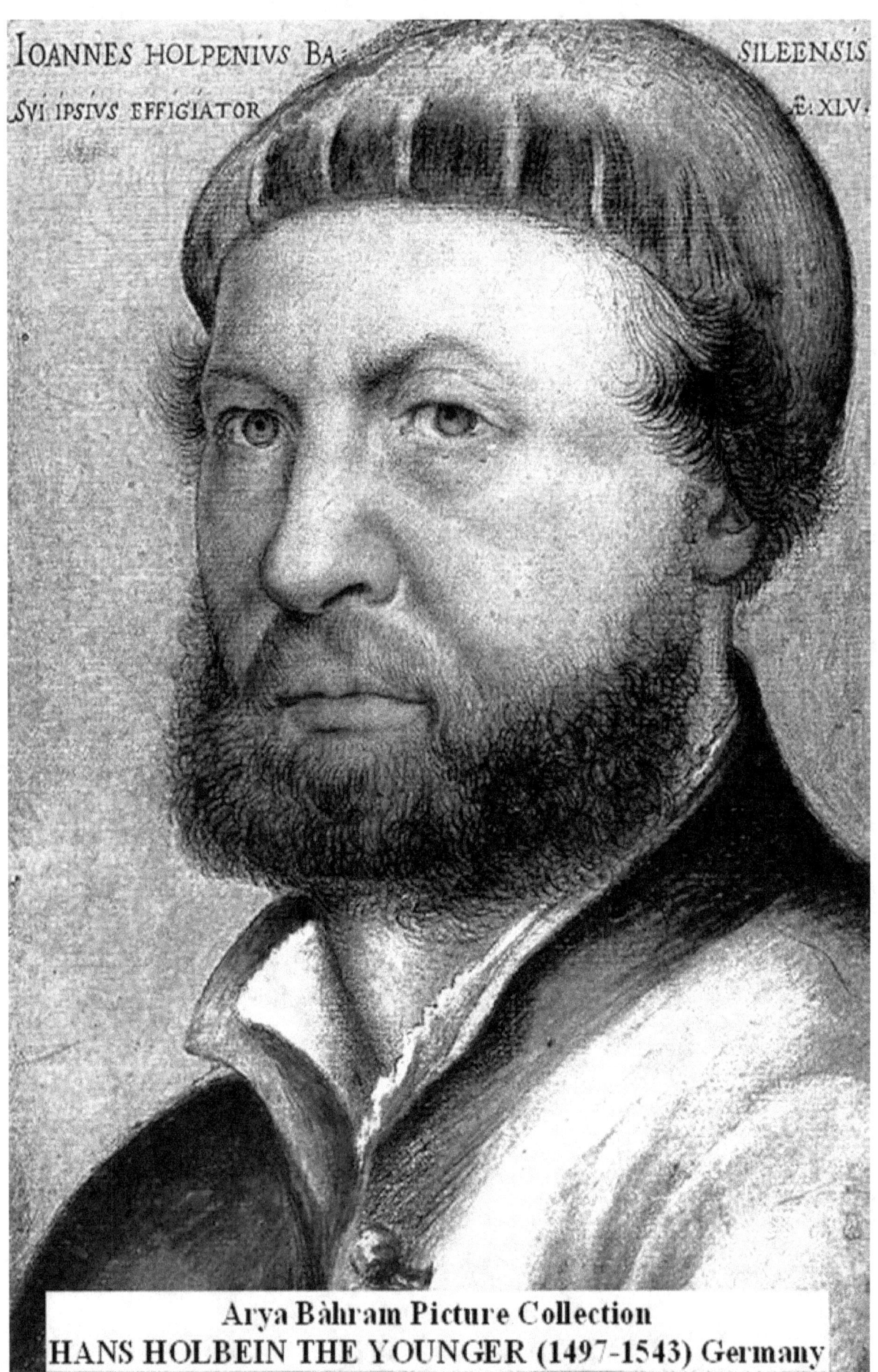

IOANNES HOLPENIVS BA· SILEENSIS

SVI IPSIVS EFFIGIATOR Æ·XLV·

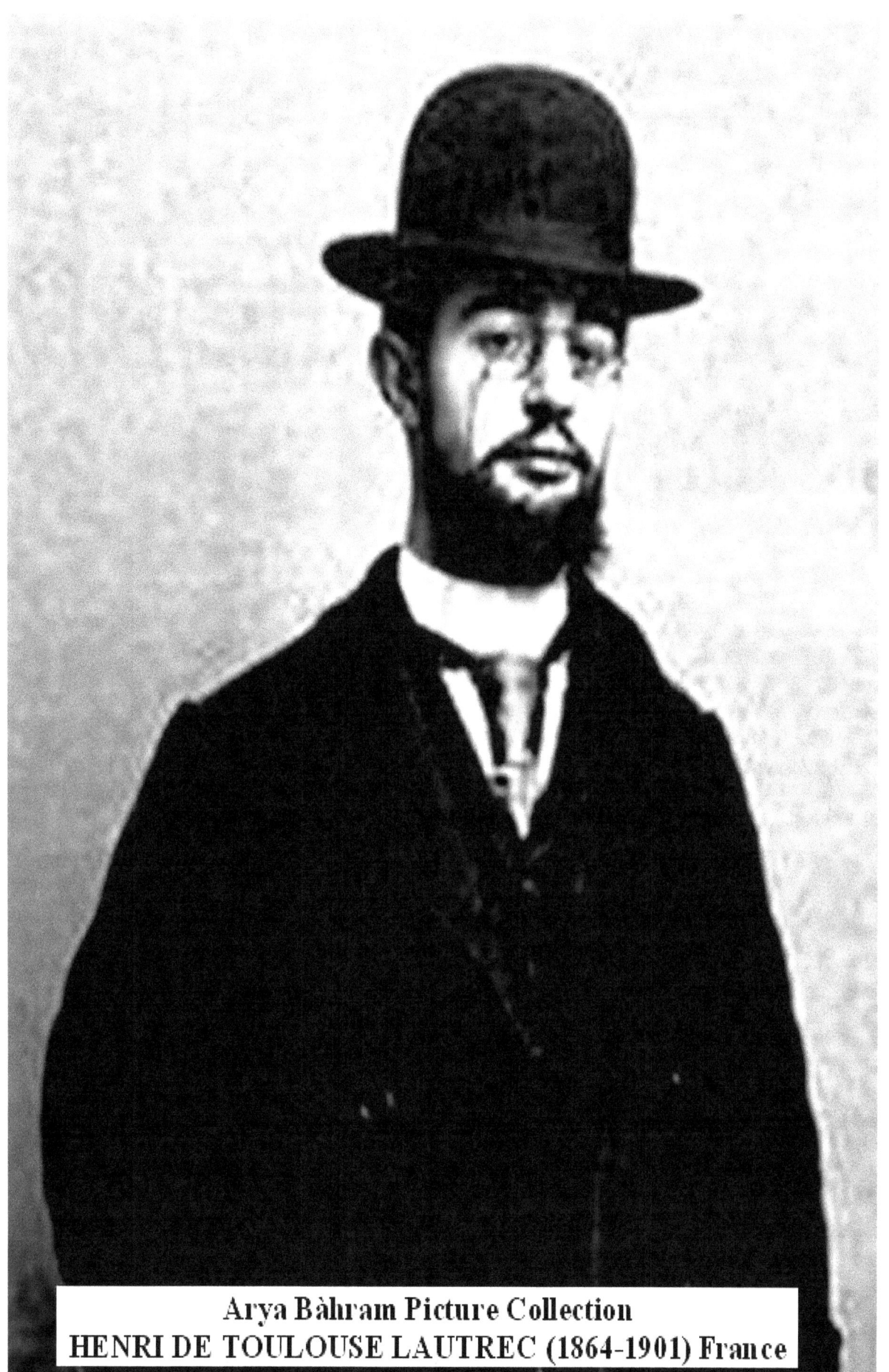

HENRI DE TOULOUSE LAUTREC (1864-1901) France

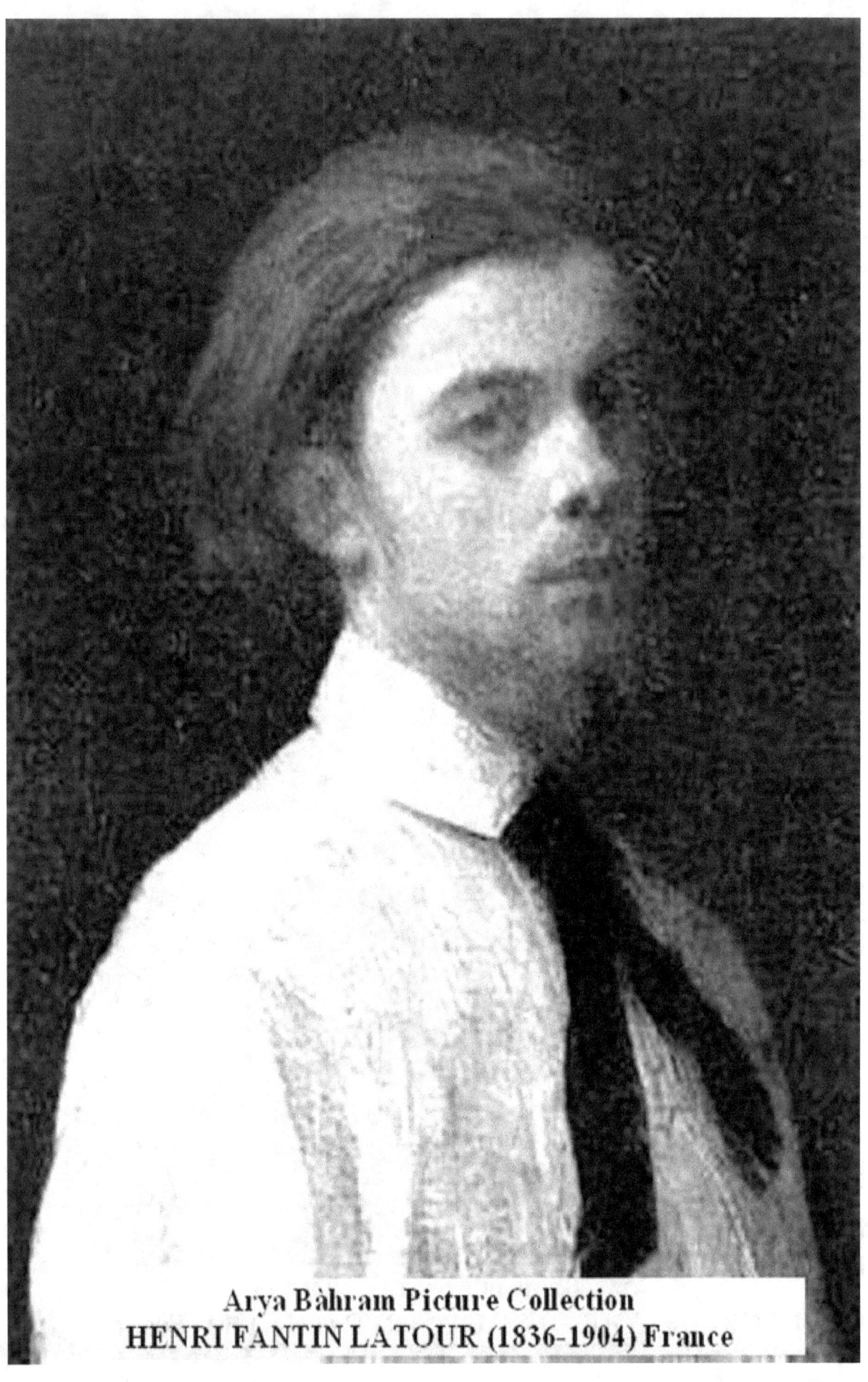

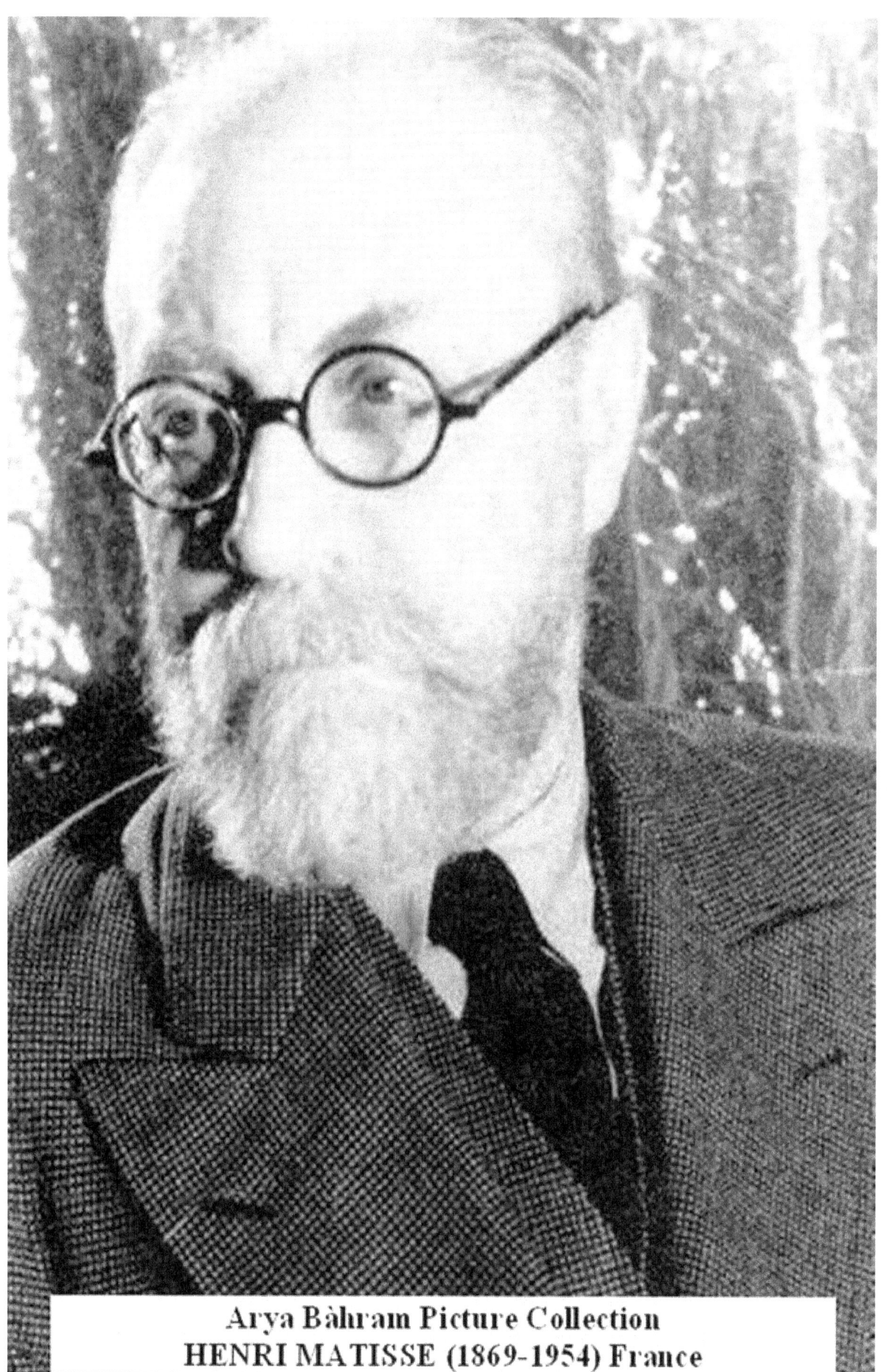

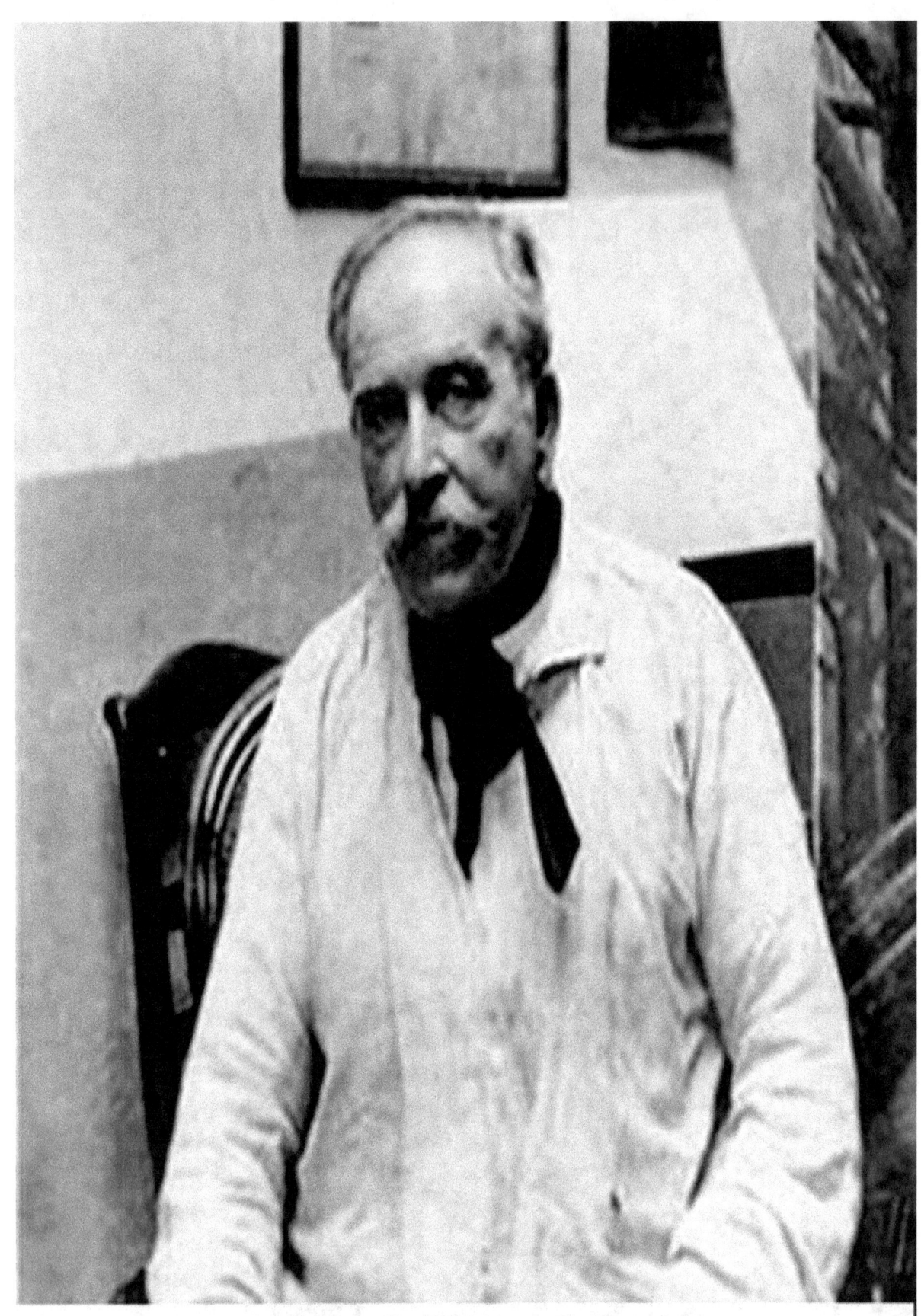

HENRI ROUSSEAU (1844-1910) France

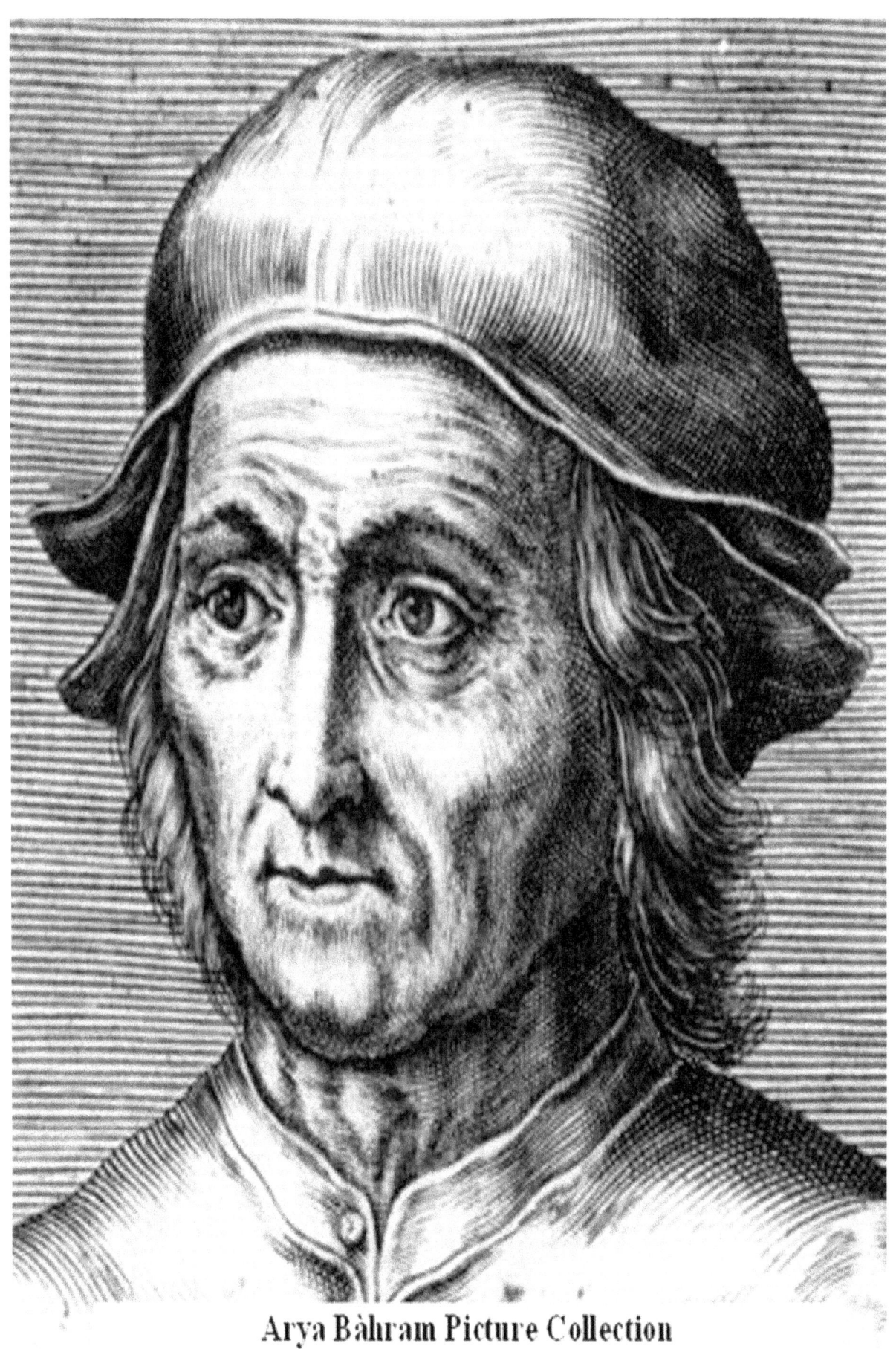

HIERONYMUS BOSCH (1450-1516) Netherland

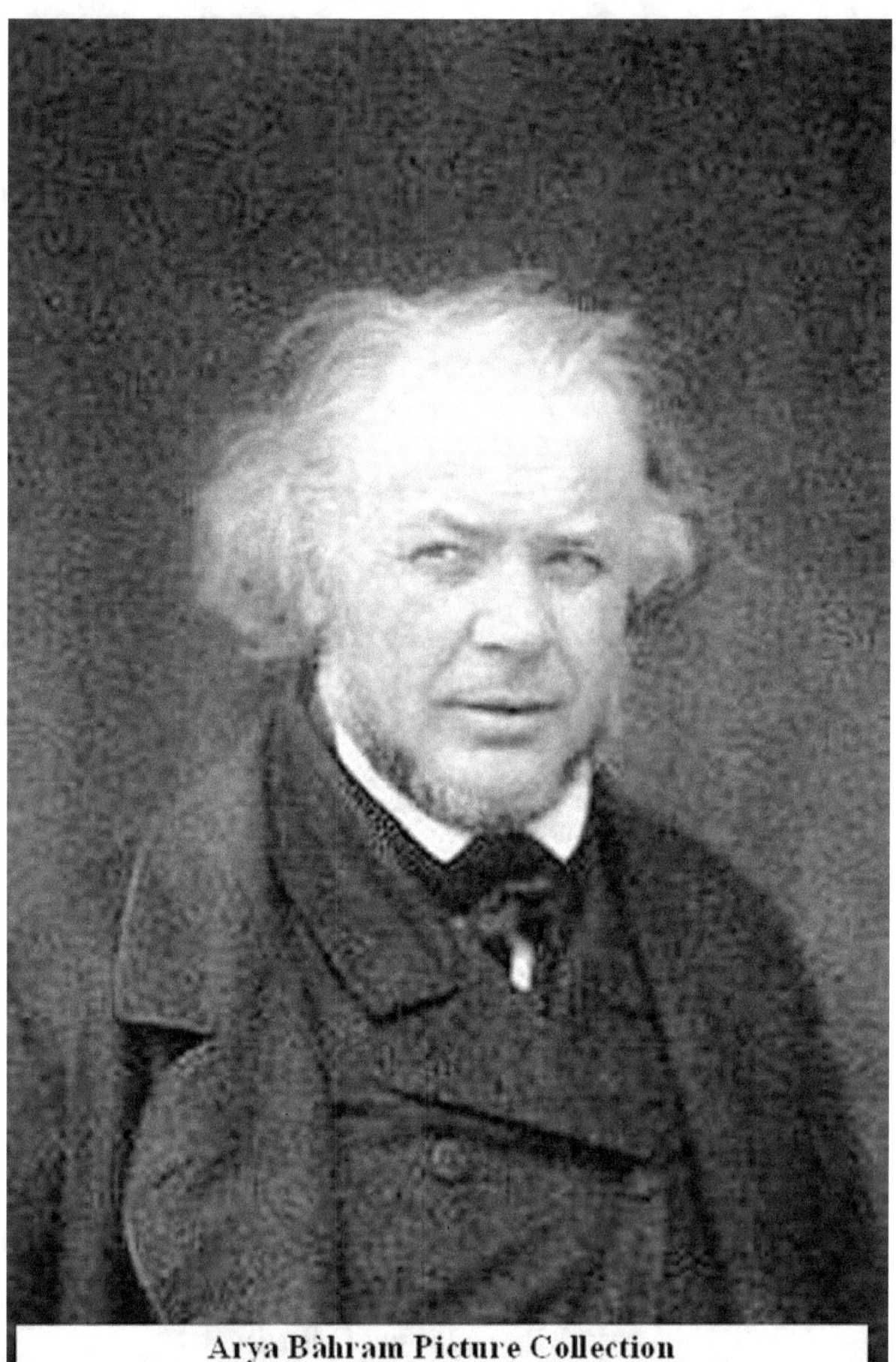

Arya Bàhram Picture Collection
HONORE DAUMIER (1808-1879) France

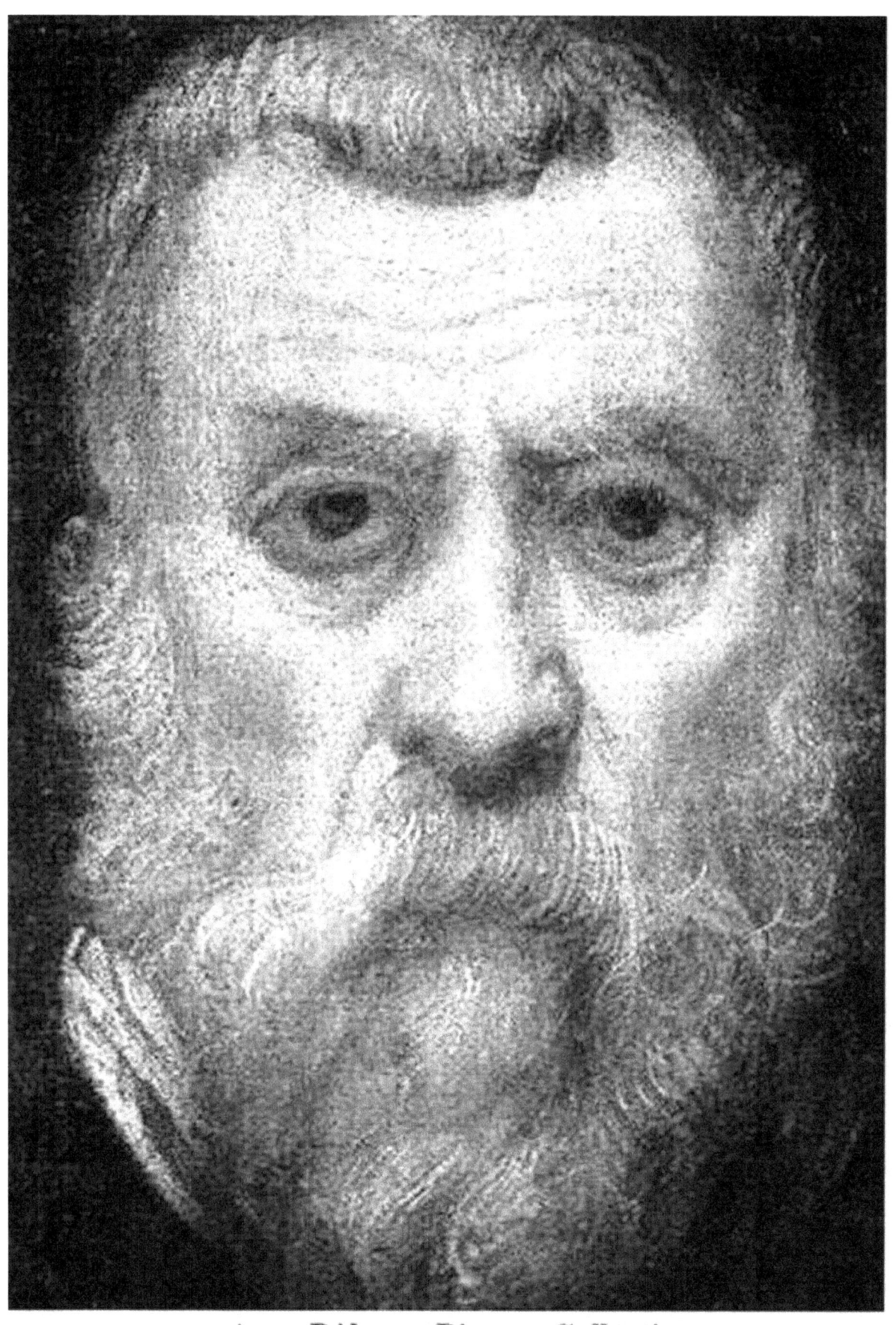

Arya Bàhram Picture Collection
JACOPO TINTORETTO (1518-1594) Italy

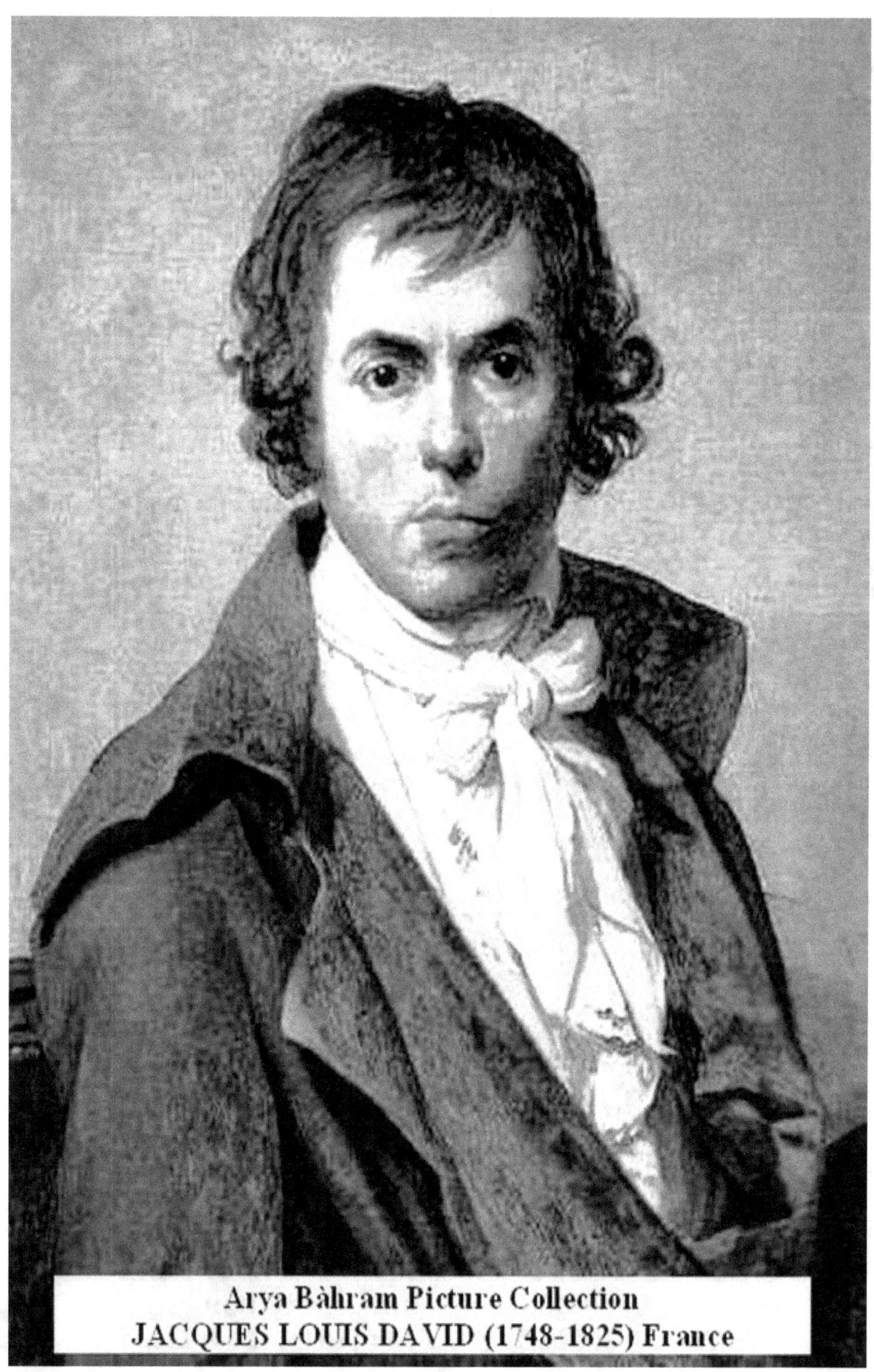

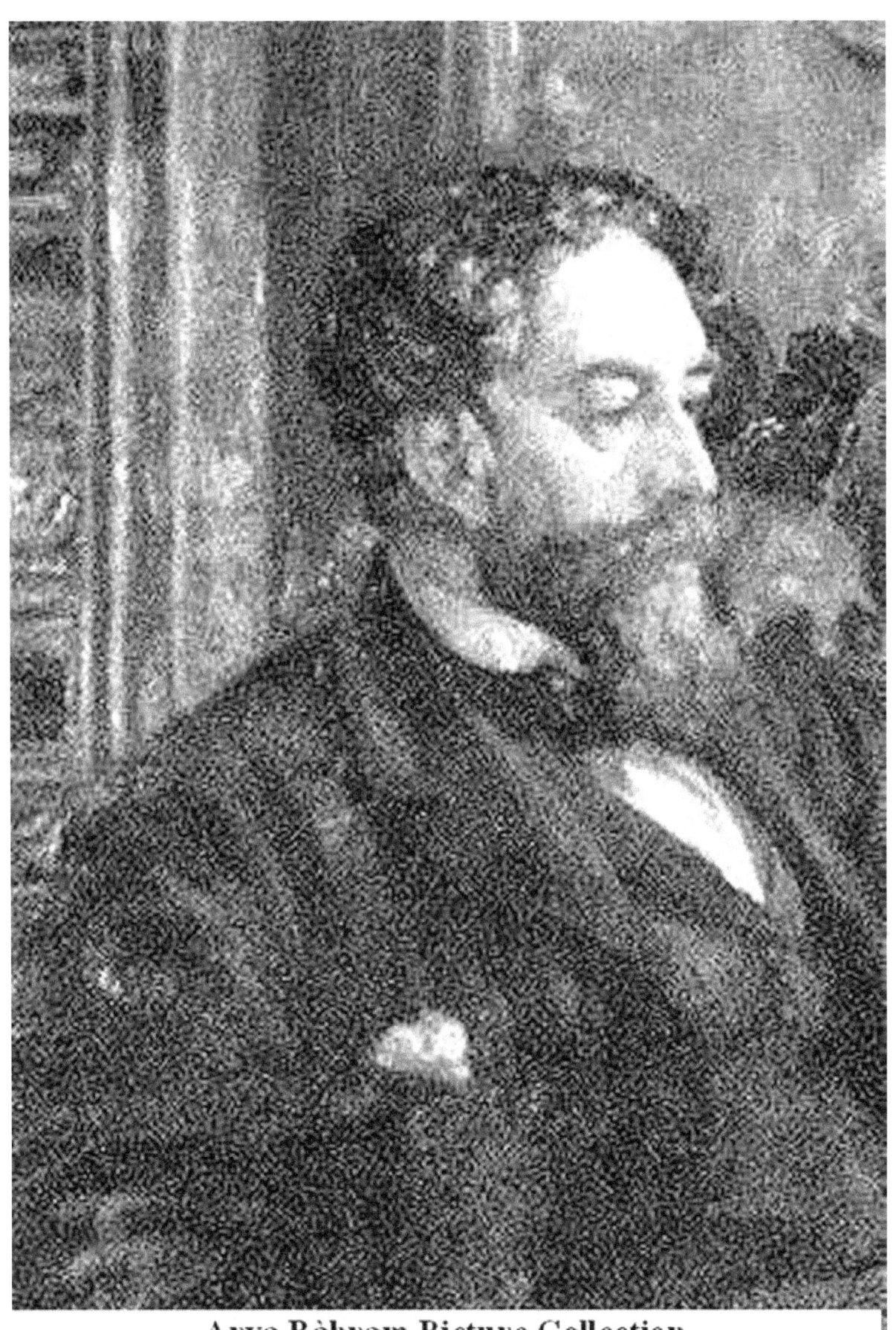

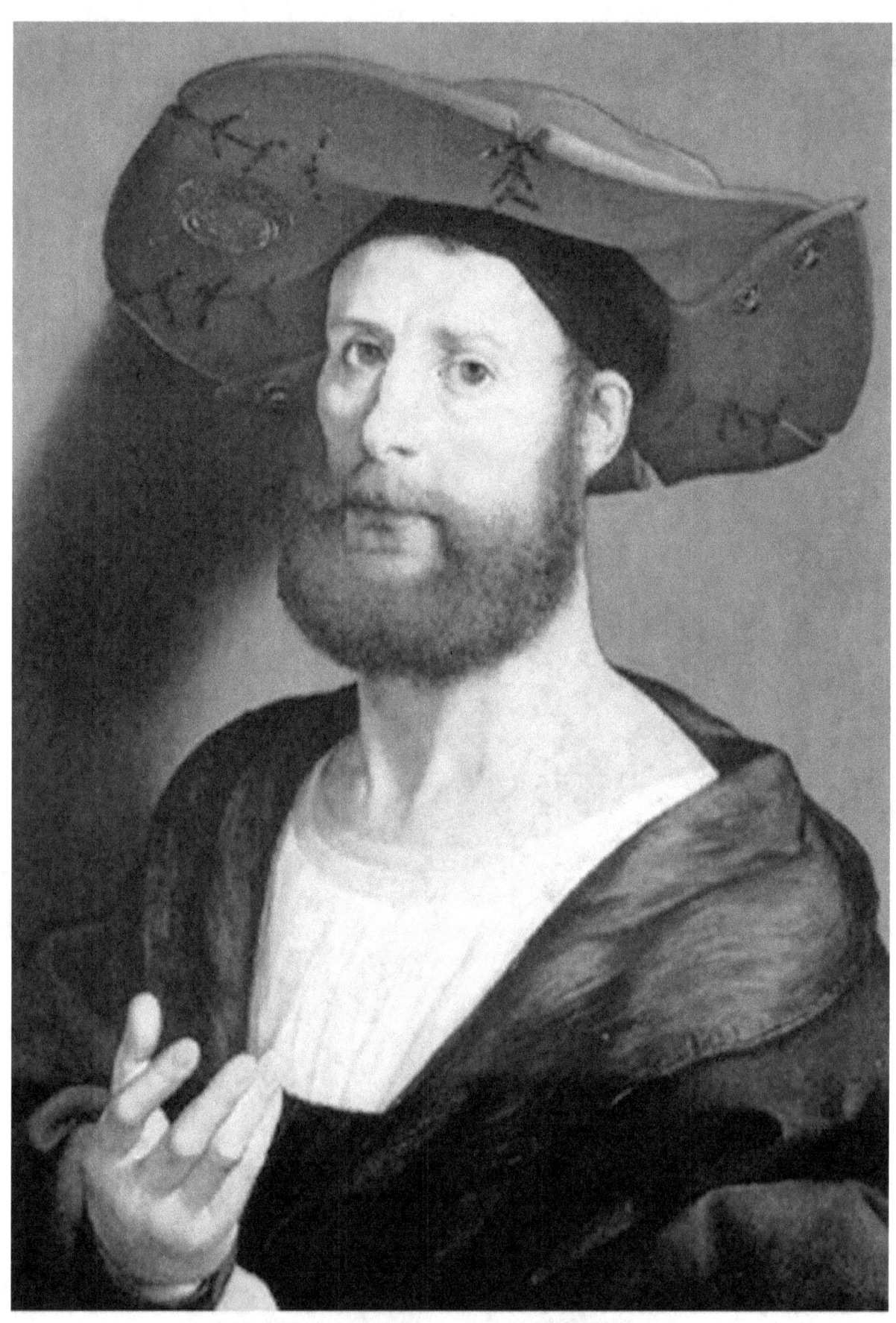

Arya Bàhram Picture Collection
JAN GOSSEAERT (1478-1532) Netherland

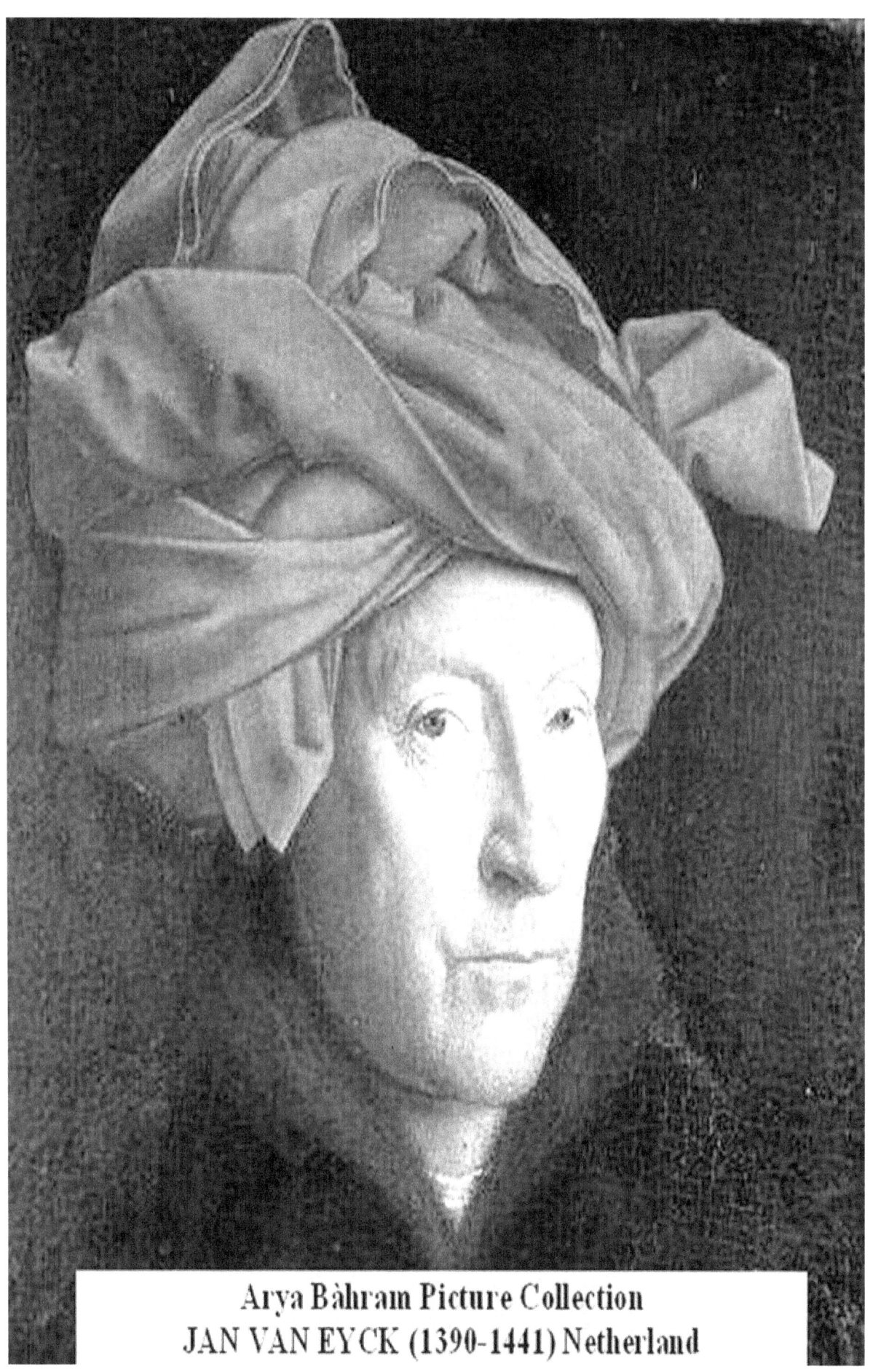

Arya Bàhram Picture Collection
JAN VAN EYCK (1390-1441) Netherland

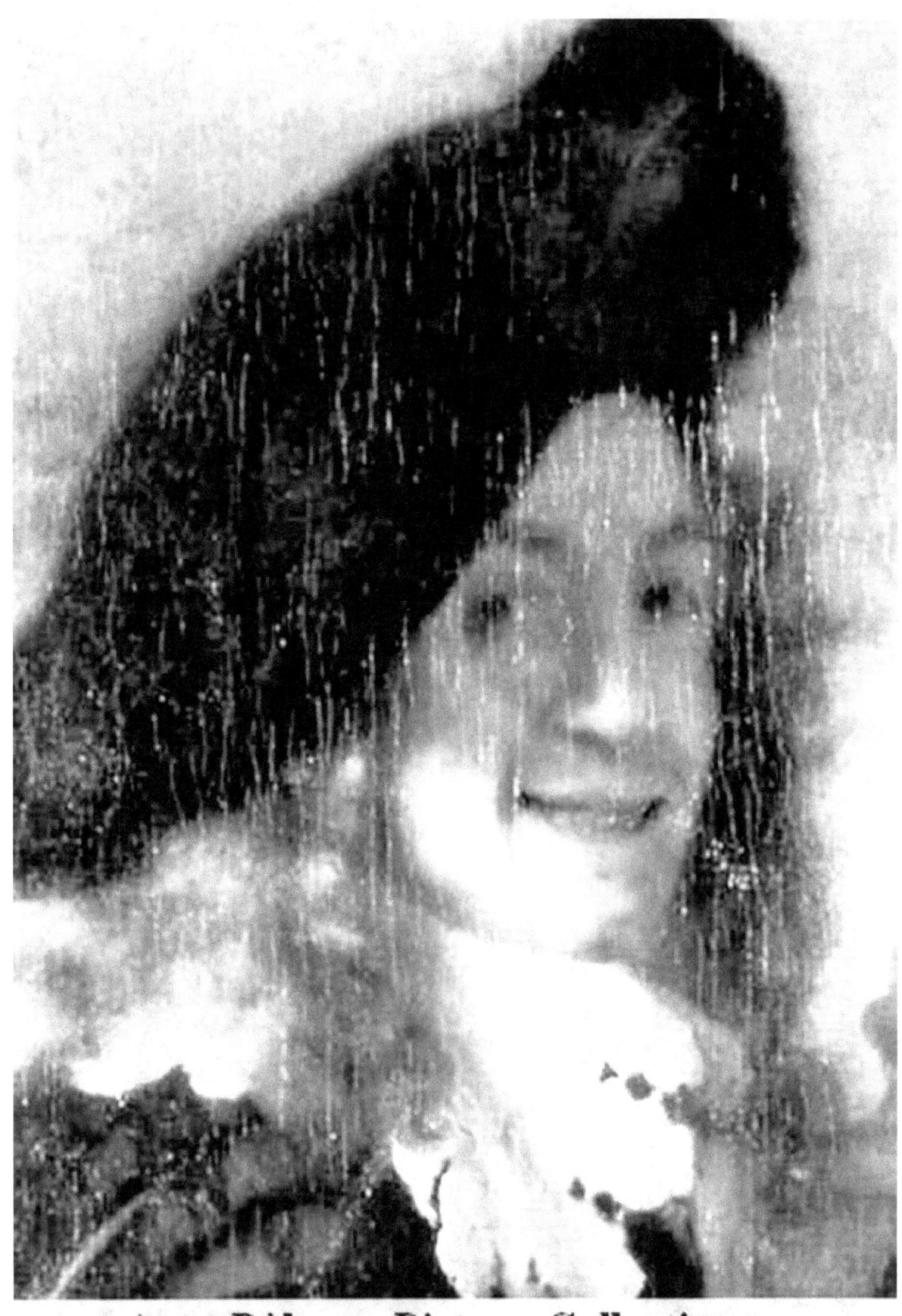

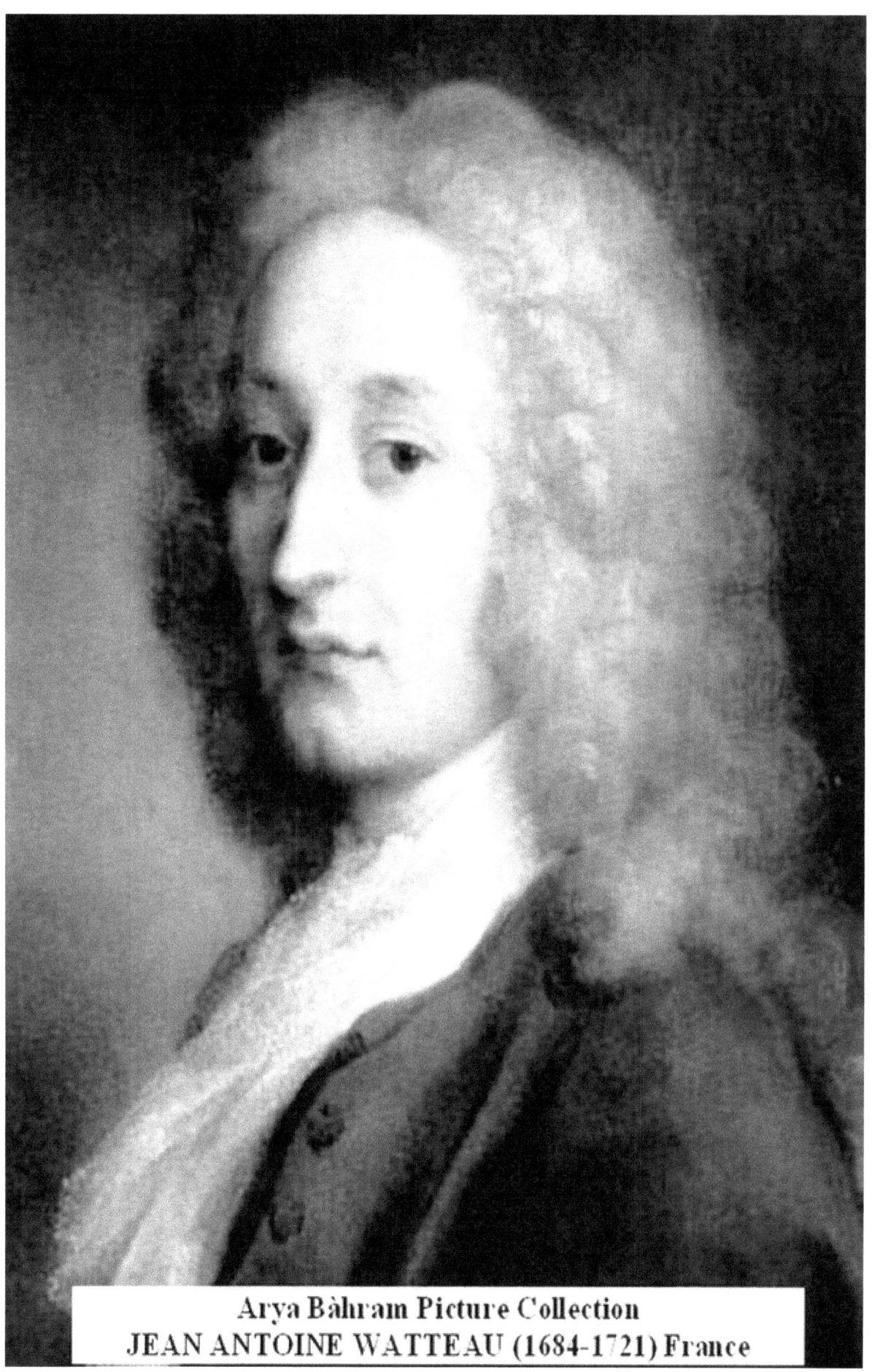

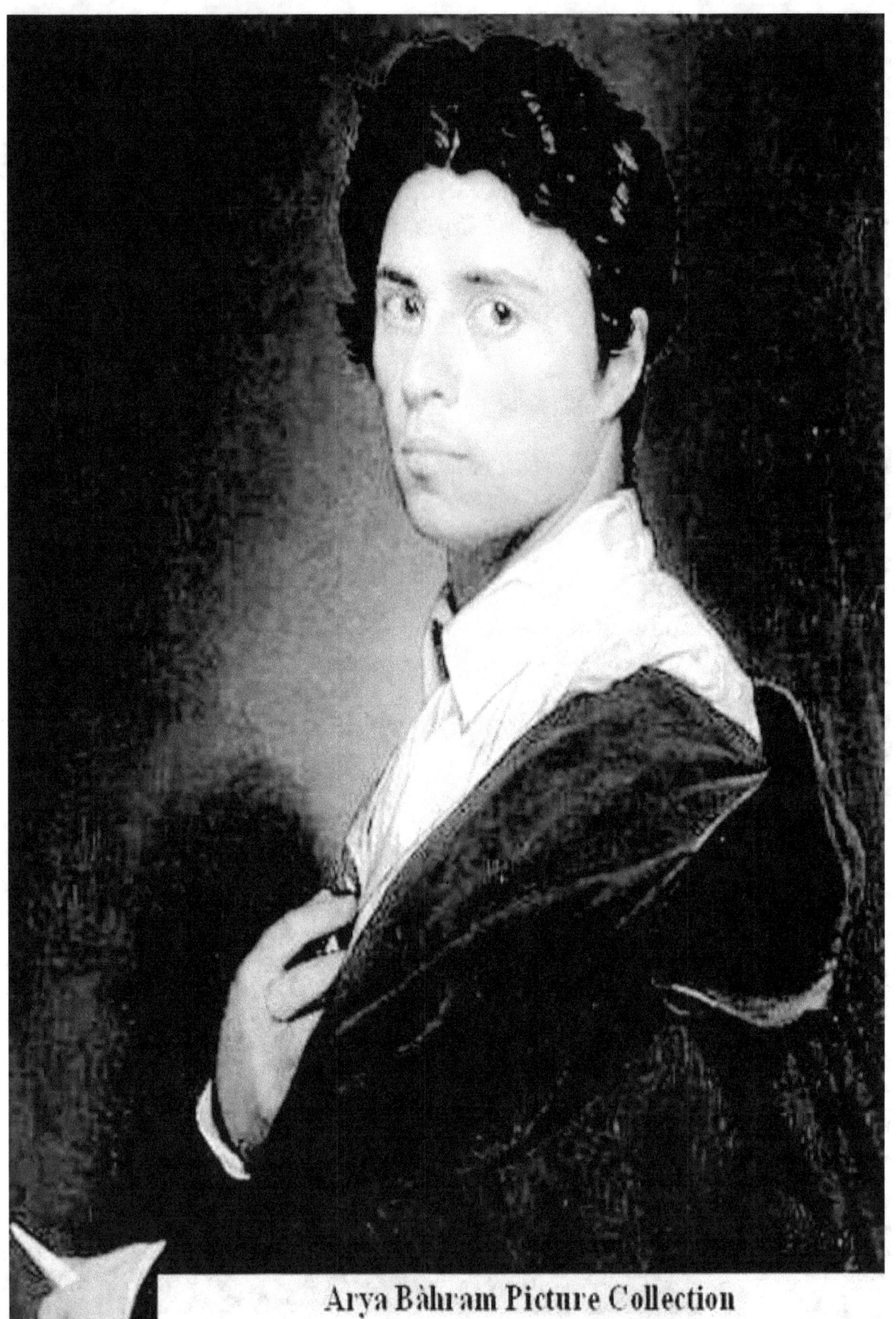

Arya Bàhram Picture Collection
JEAN AUGUSTE DOMINIQUE INGRES (1780-1867)
France

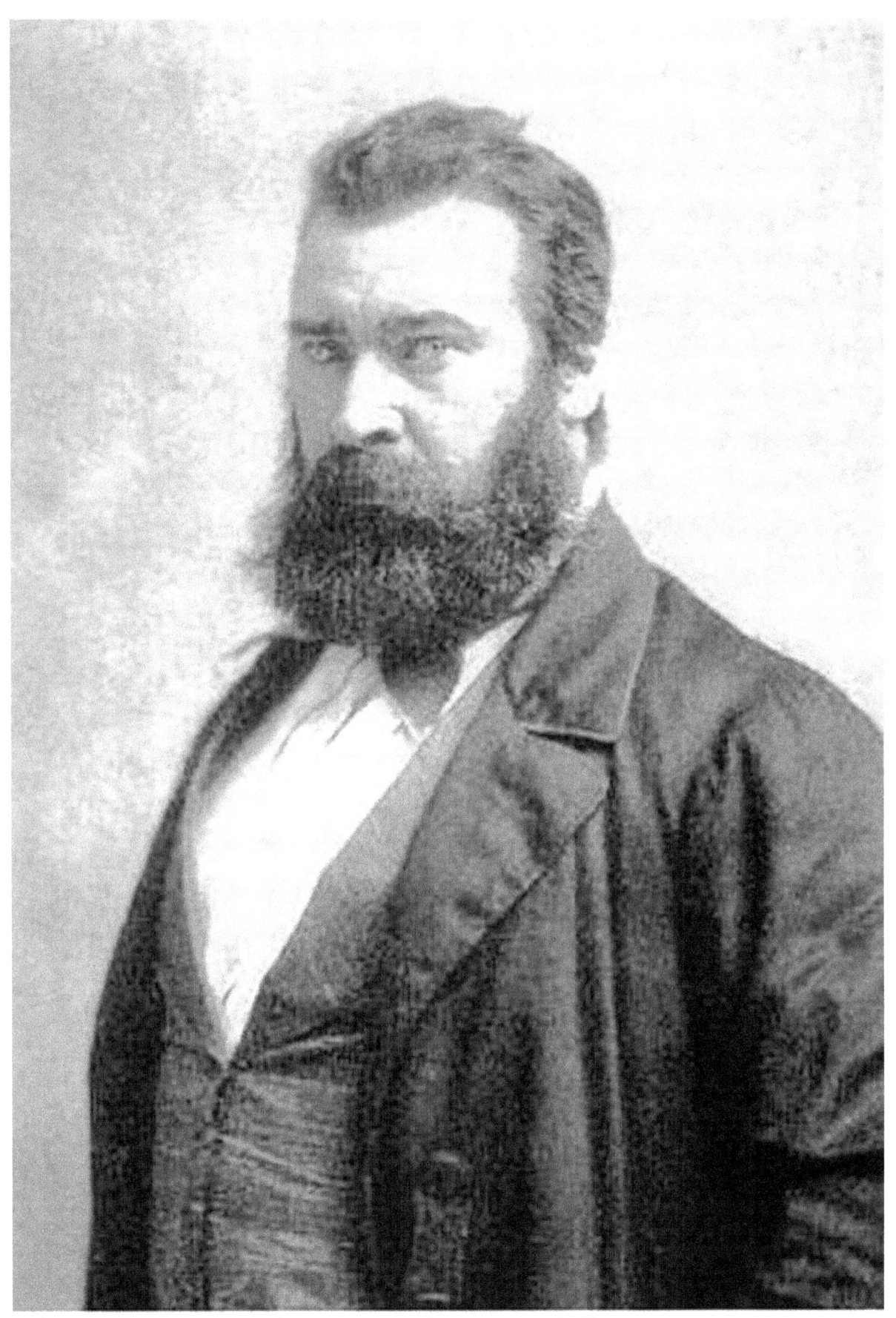

JEAN FRANÇOIS MILLET (1814-1875) France

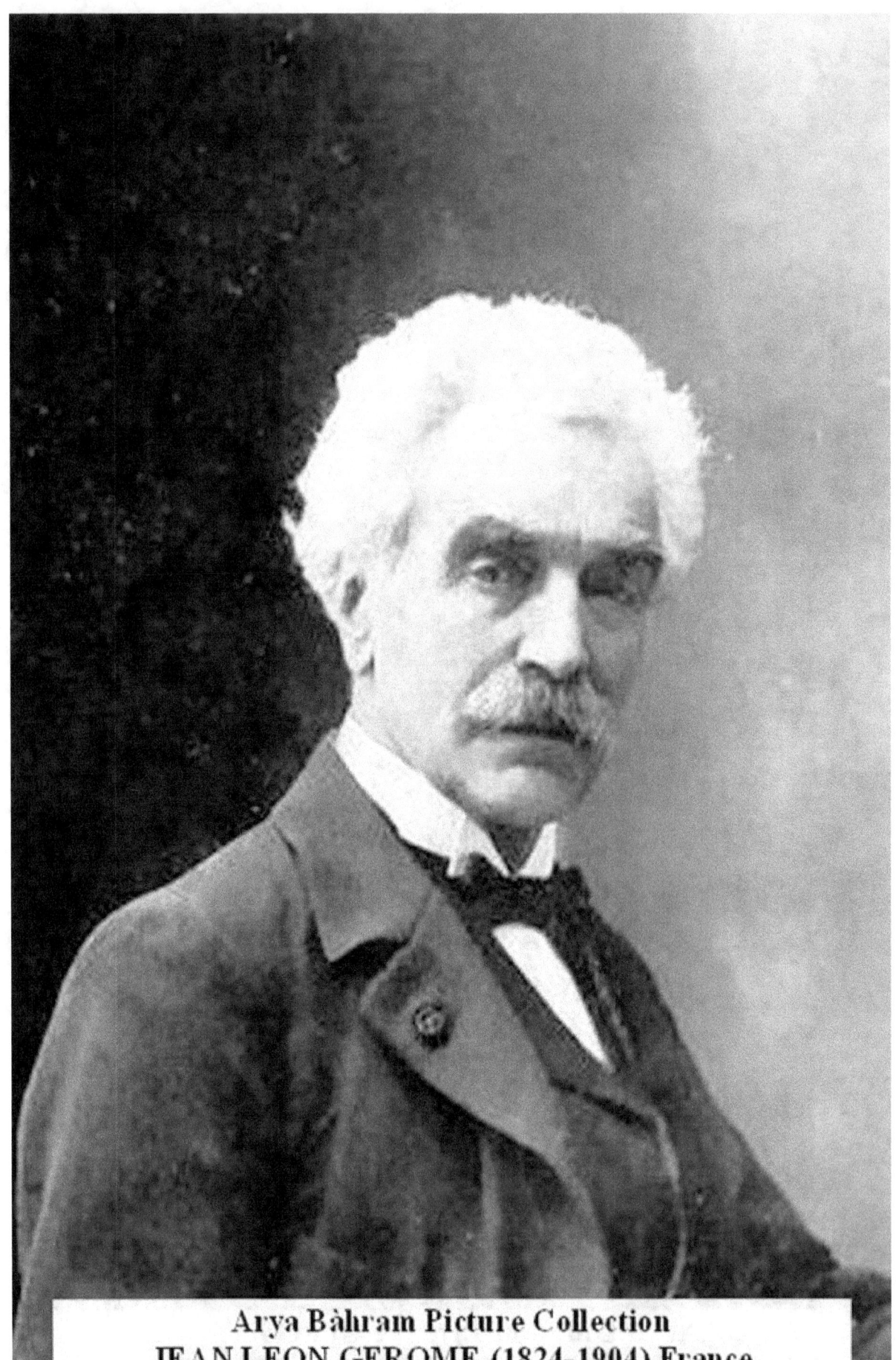

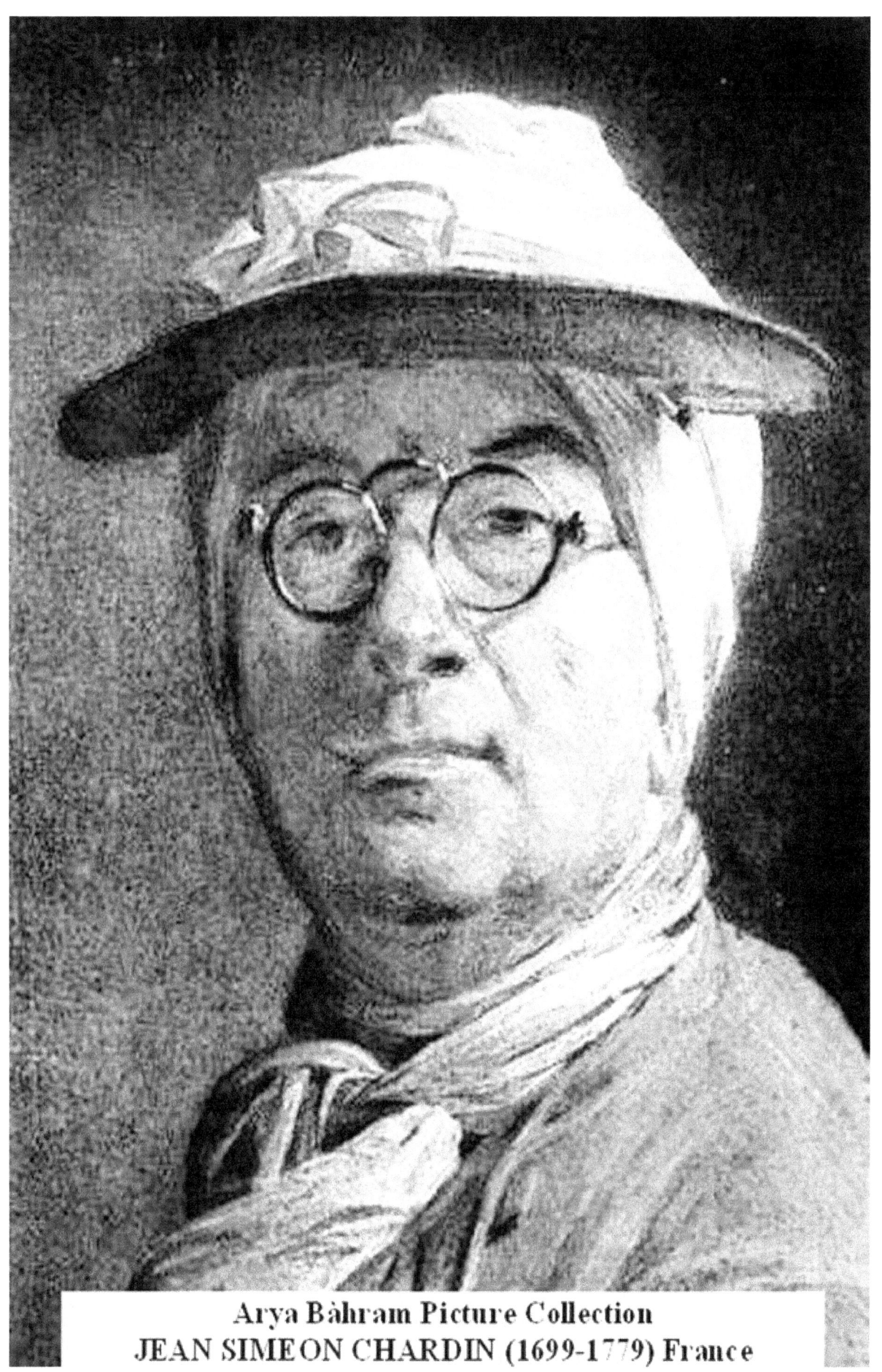

JEAN SIMEON CHARDIN (1699-1779) France

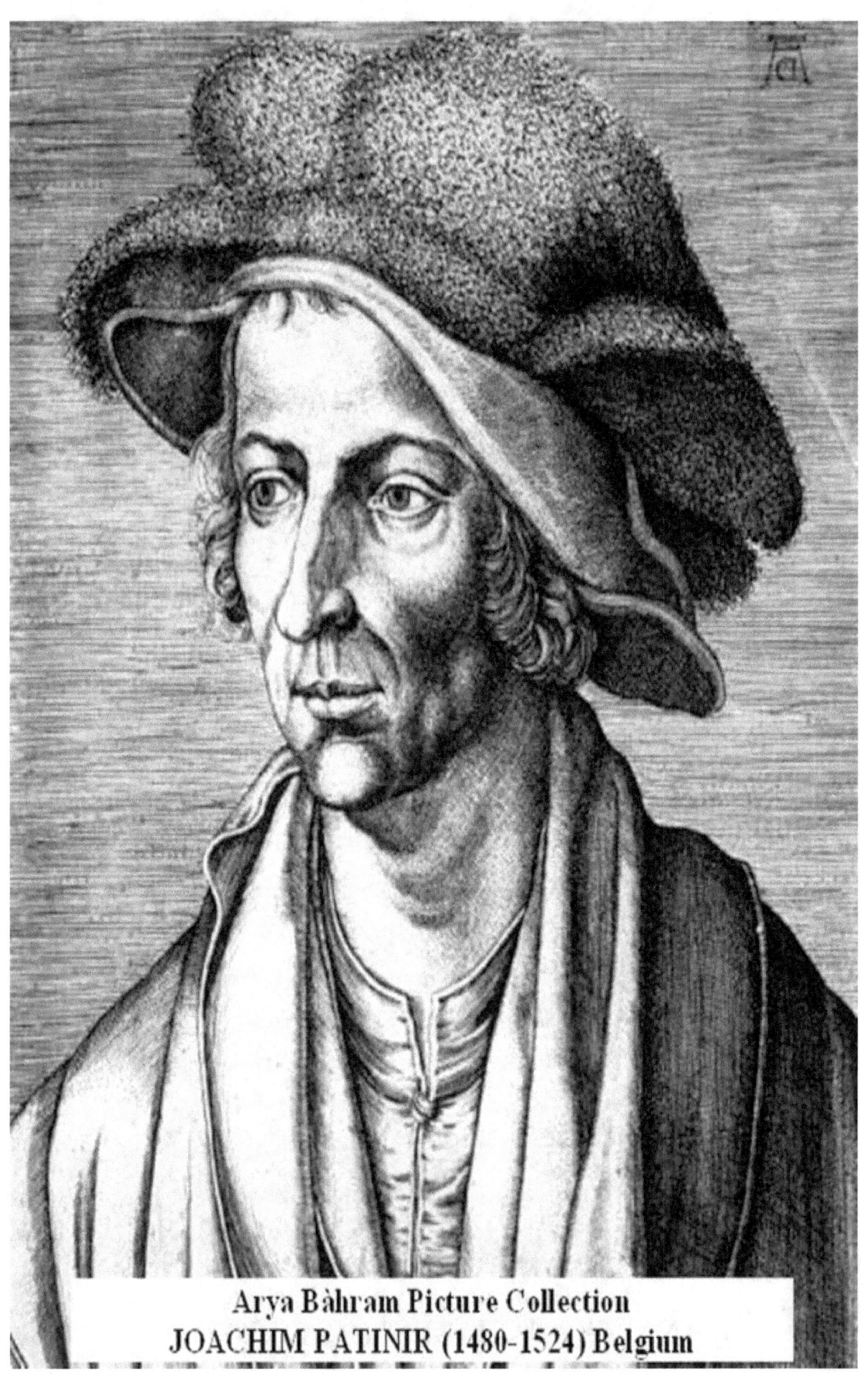

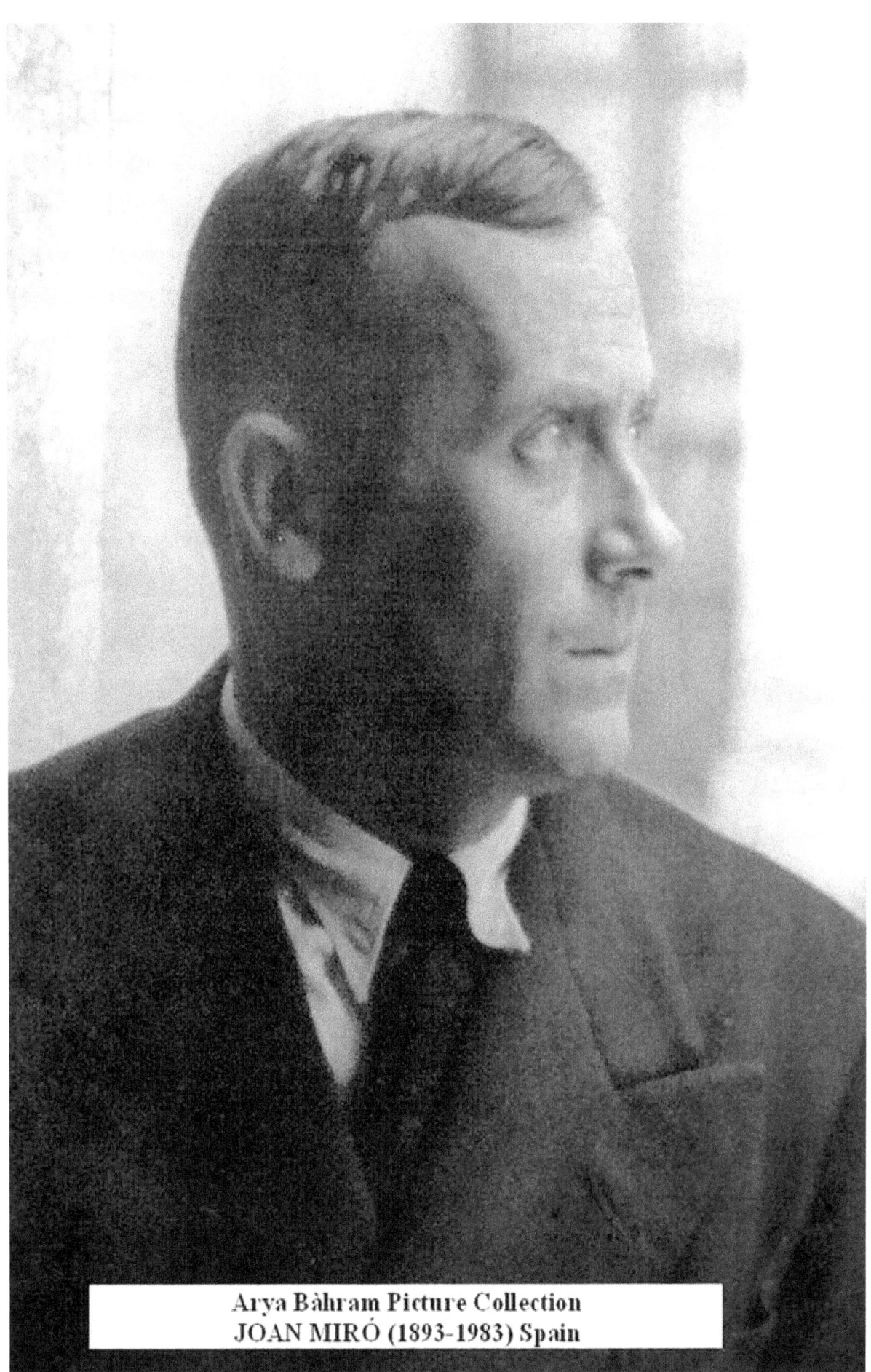

Arya Bàhram Picture Collection
JOAN MIRÓ (1893-1983) Spain

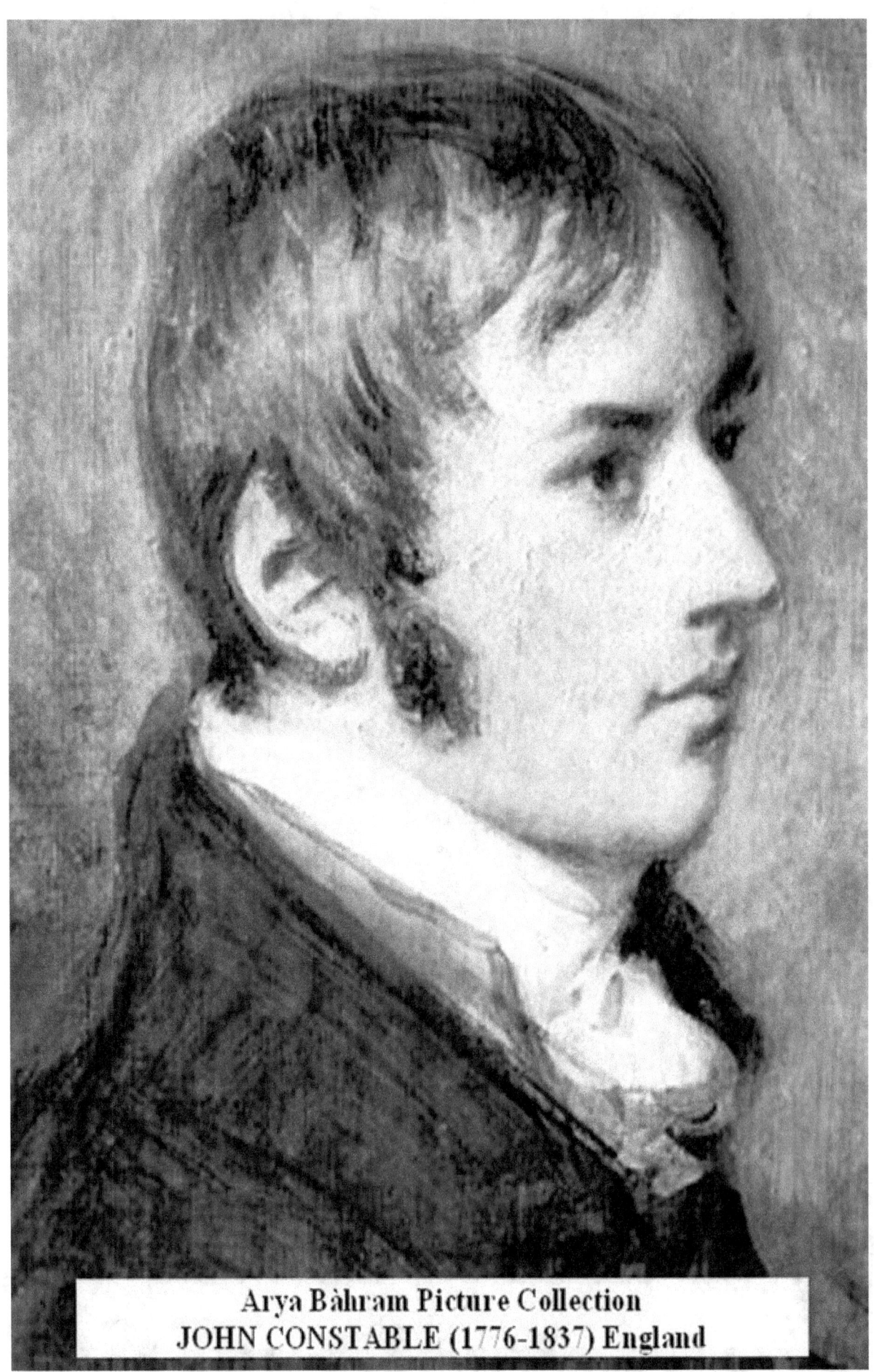

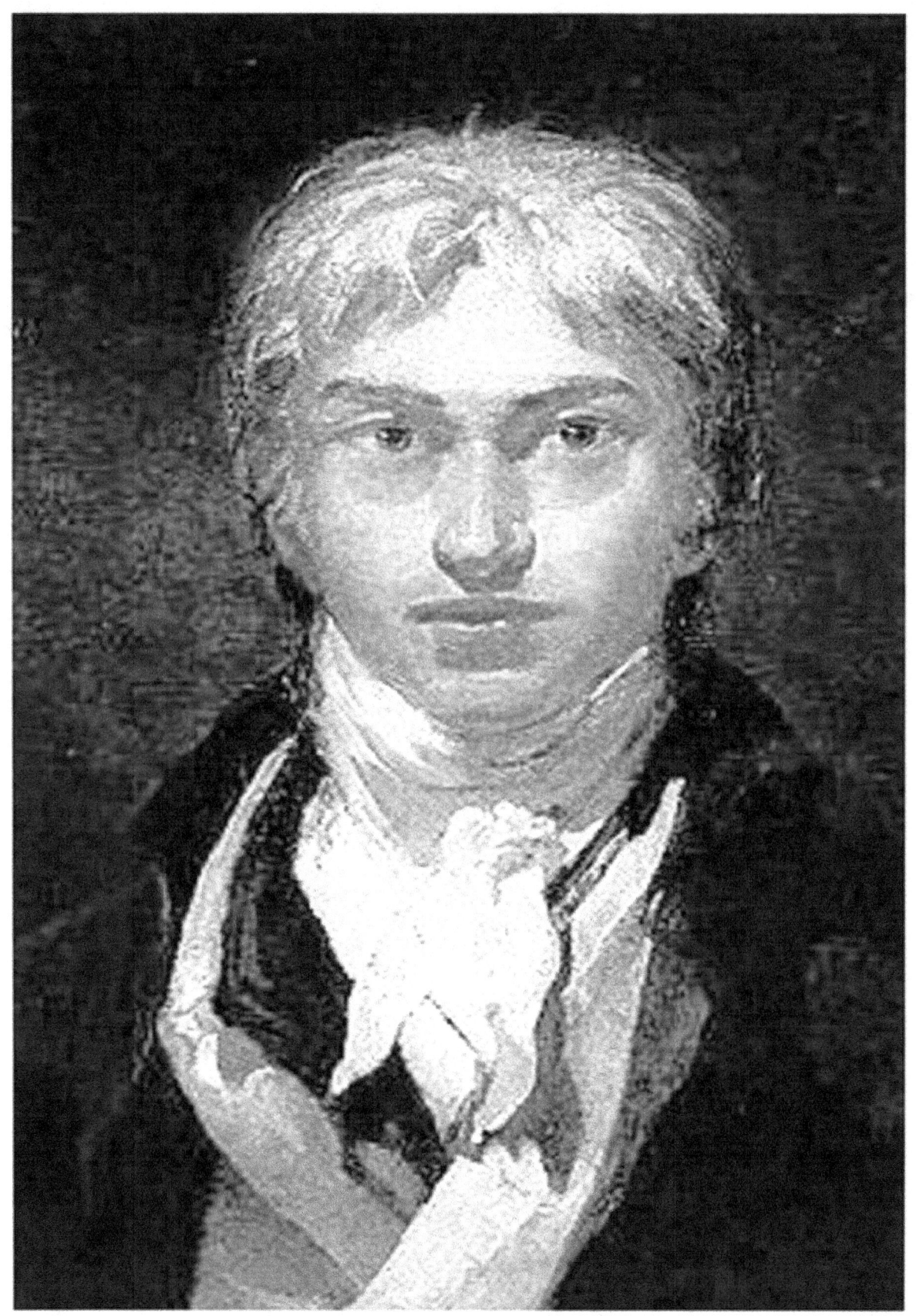

Arya Bàhram Picture Collection
JOSEPH MALLORD WILLIAM TURNER
(1775-1851) England

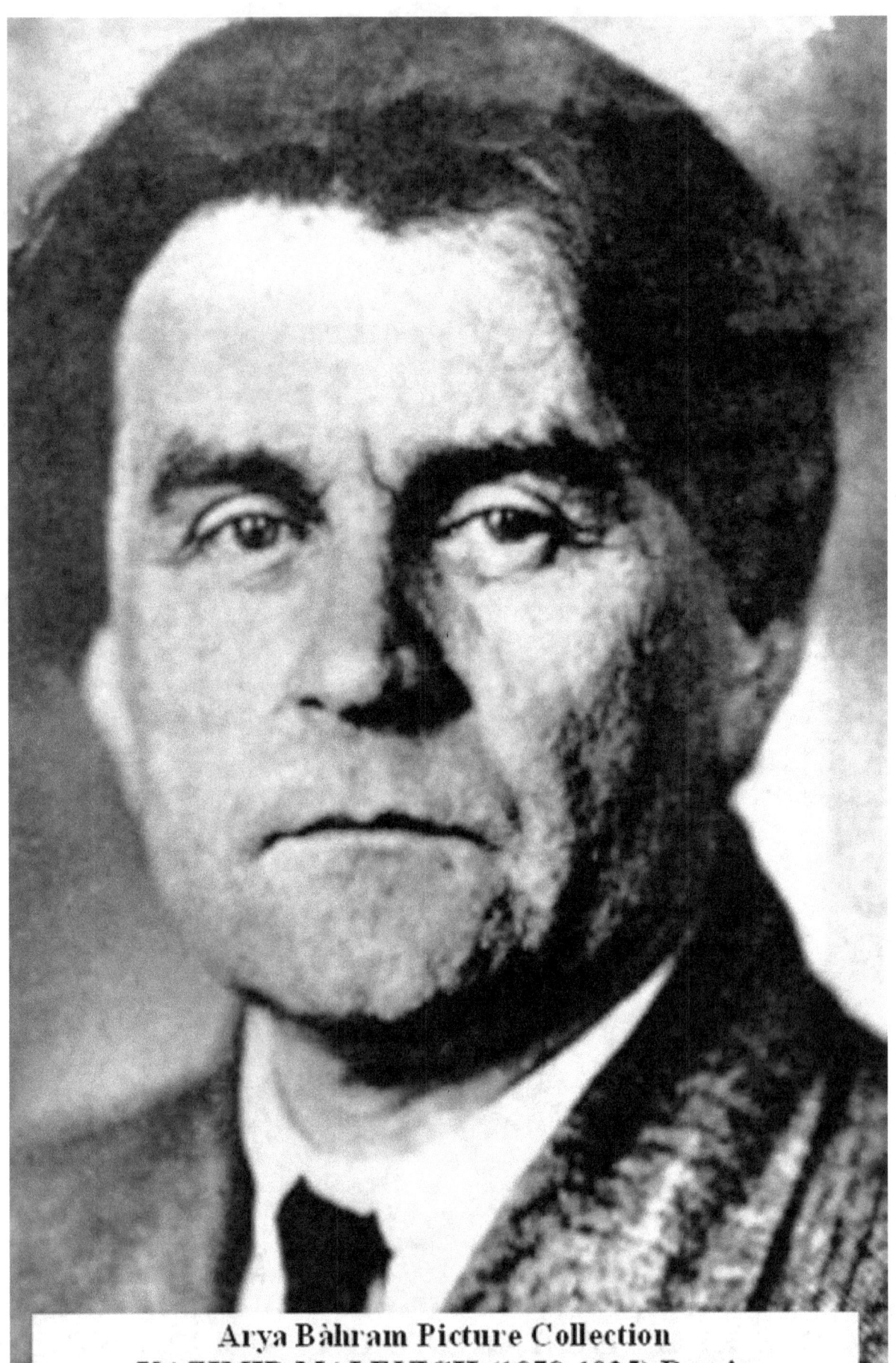

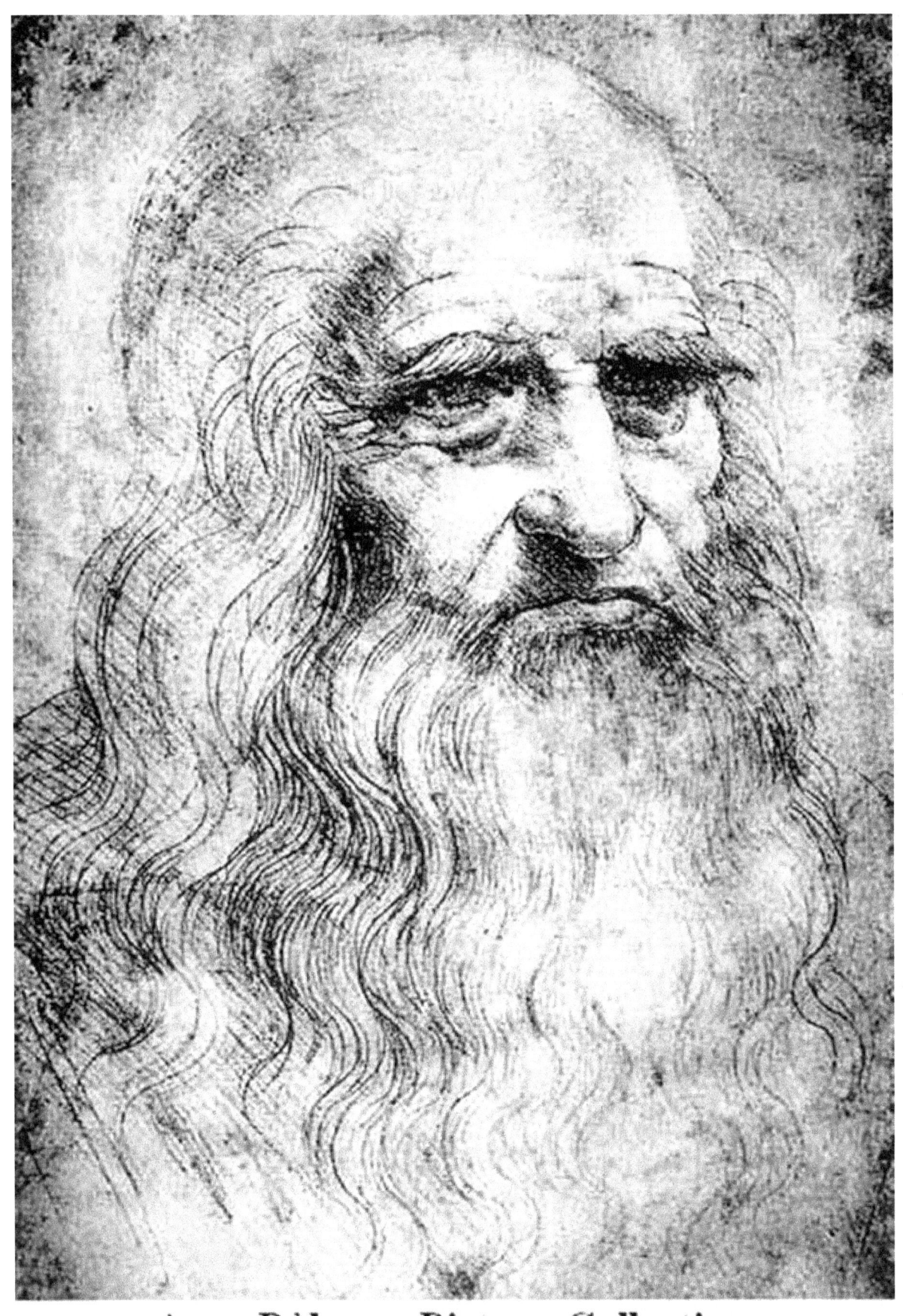

LEONARDO DA VINCI (1452-1519) Italy

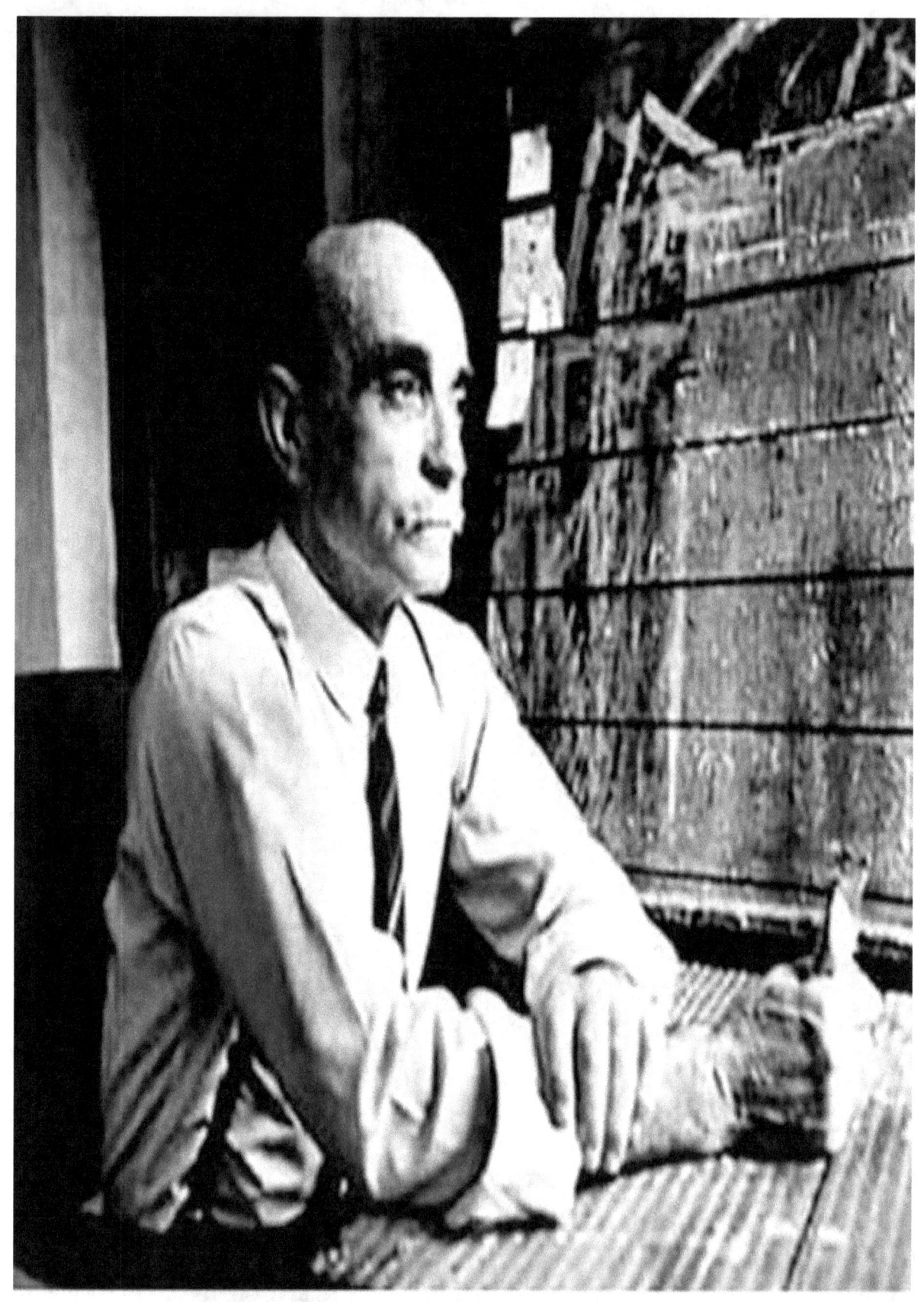

Arya Bàhram Picture Collection
LUCIO FONTANA (1899-1968) Italy

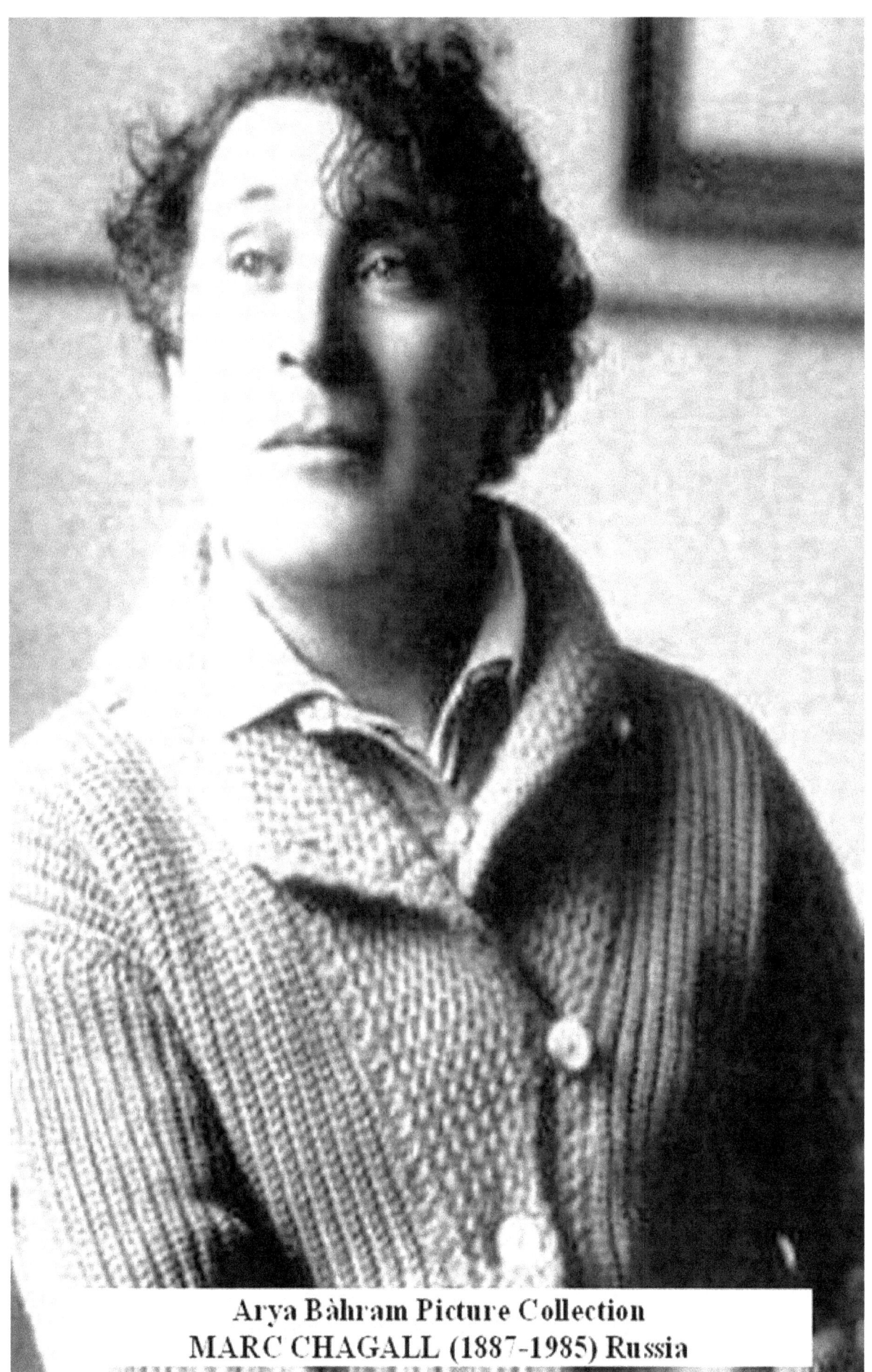

Arya Bàhram Picture Collection
MARC CHAGALL (1887-1985) Russia

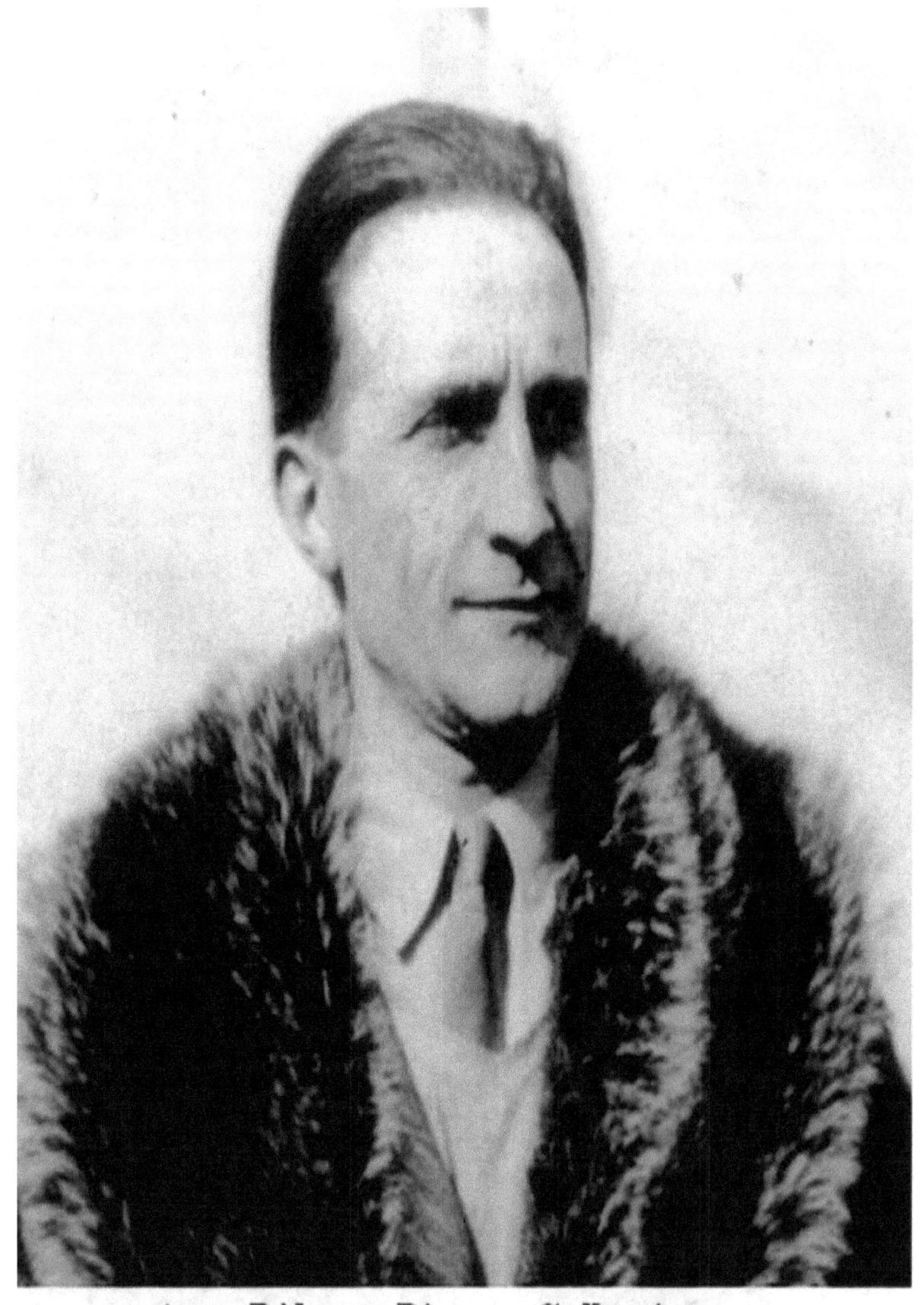

Arya Bàhram Picture Collection
MARCEL DUCHAMP (1887-1968) France

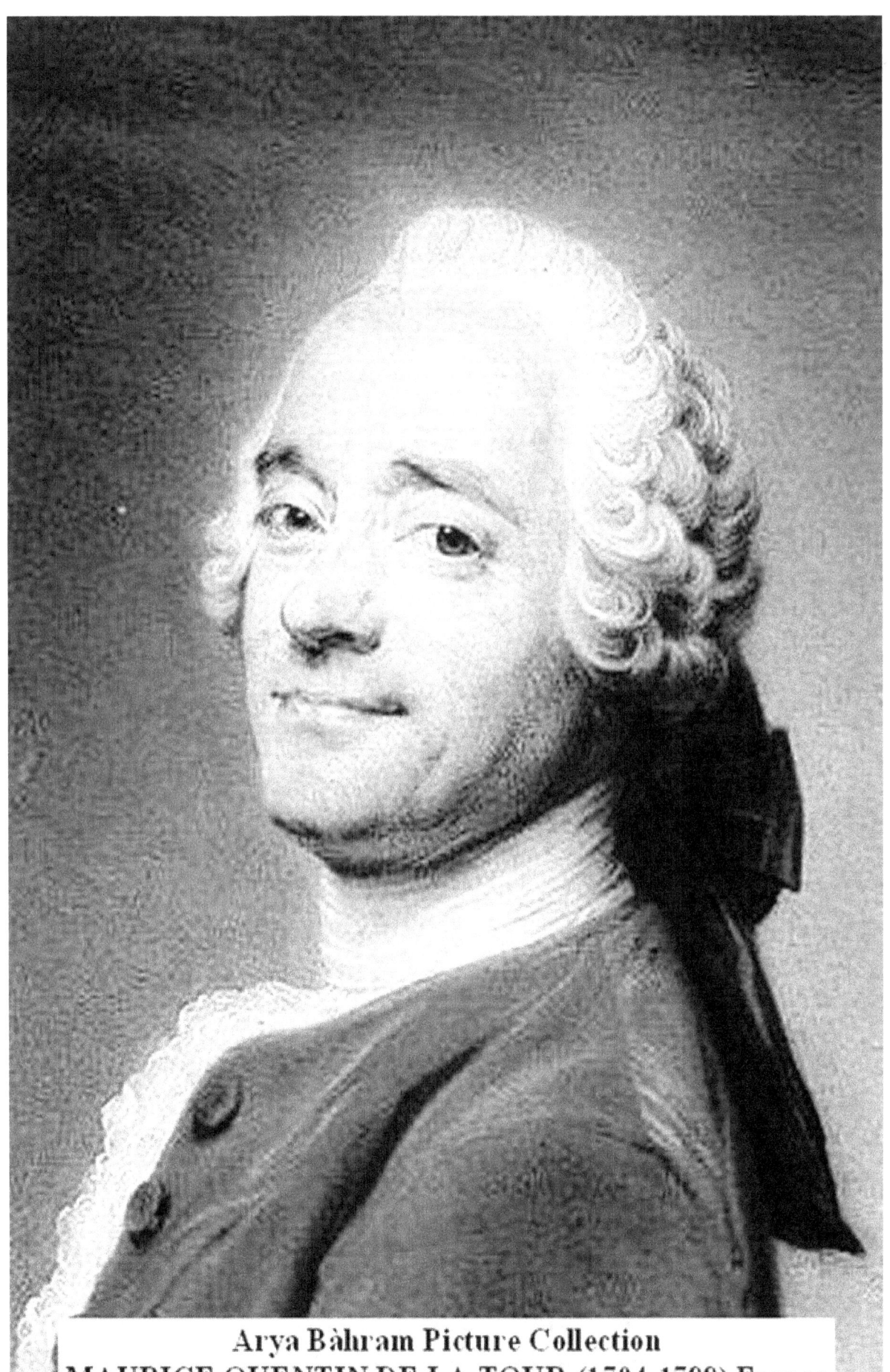

Arya Bàhram Picture Collection
MAURICE QUENTIN DE LA TOUR (1704-1788) France

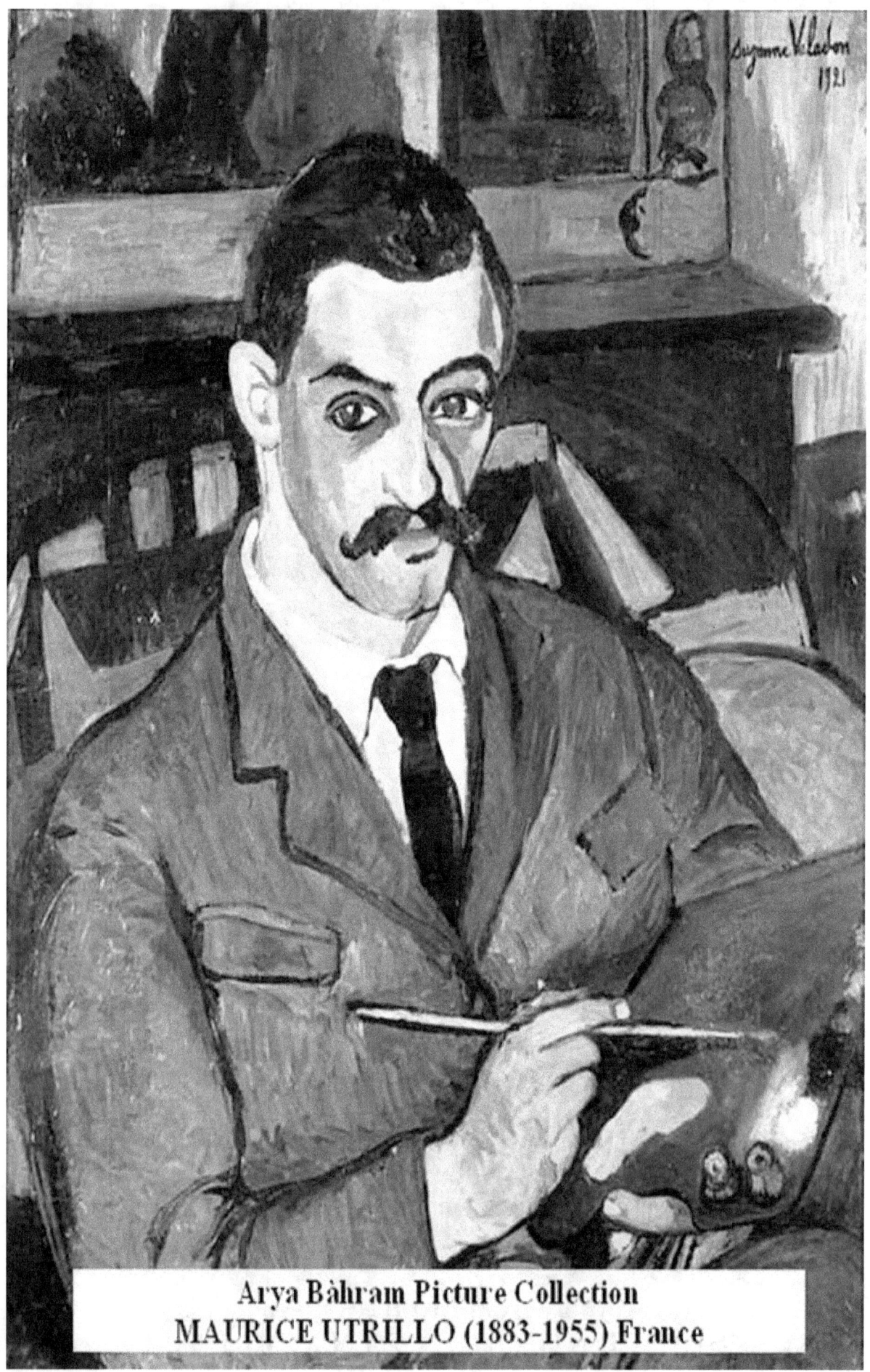

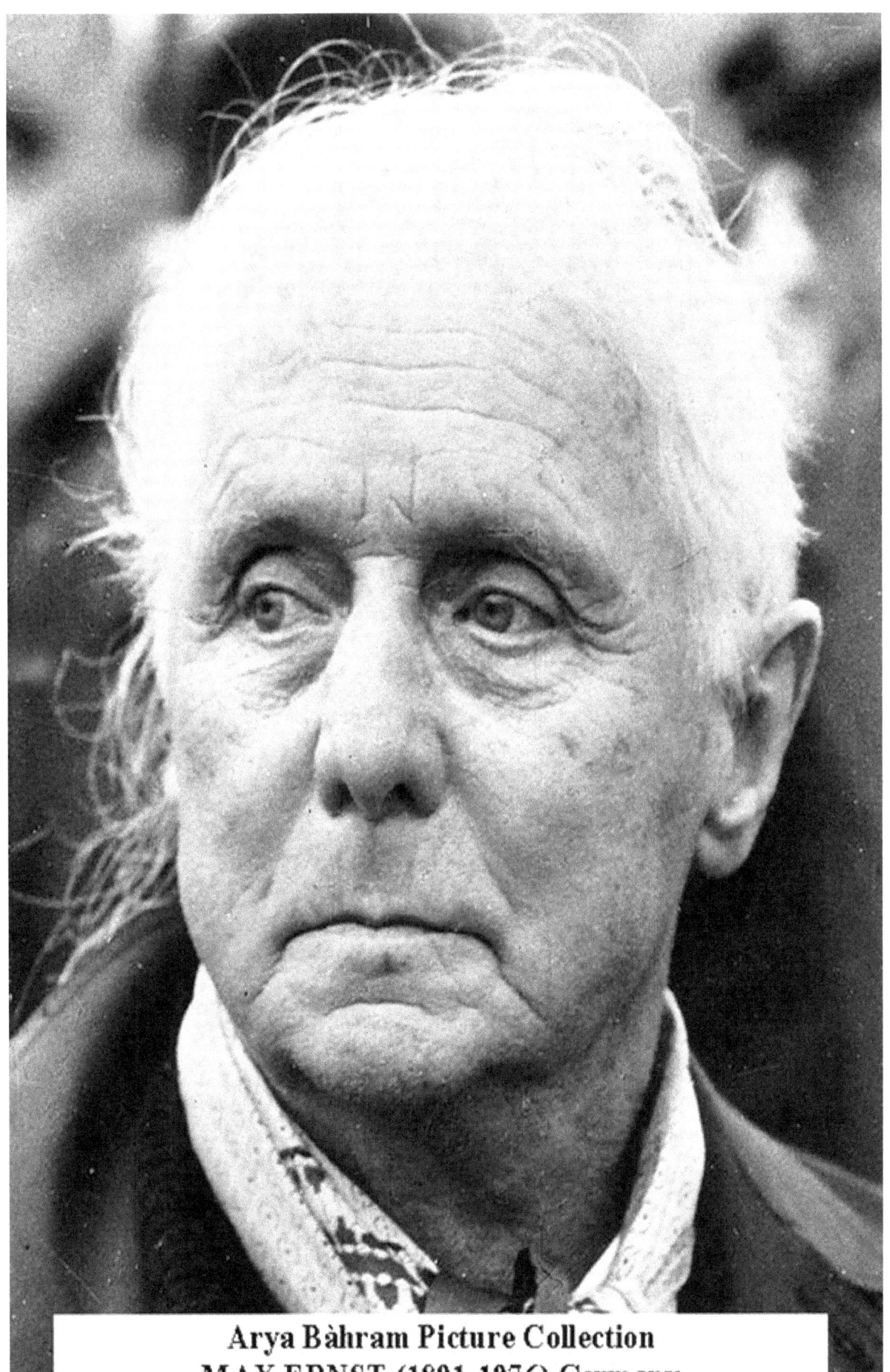

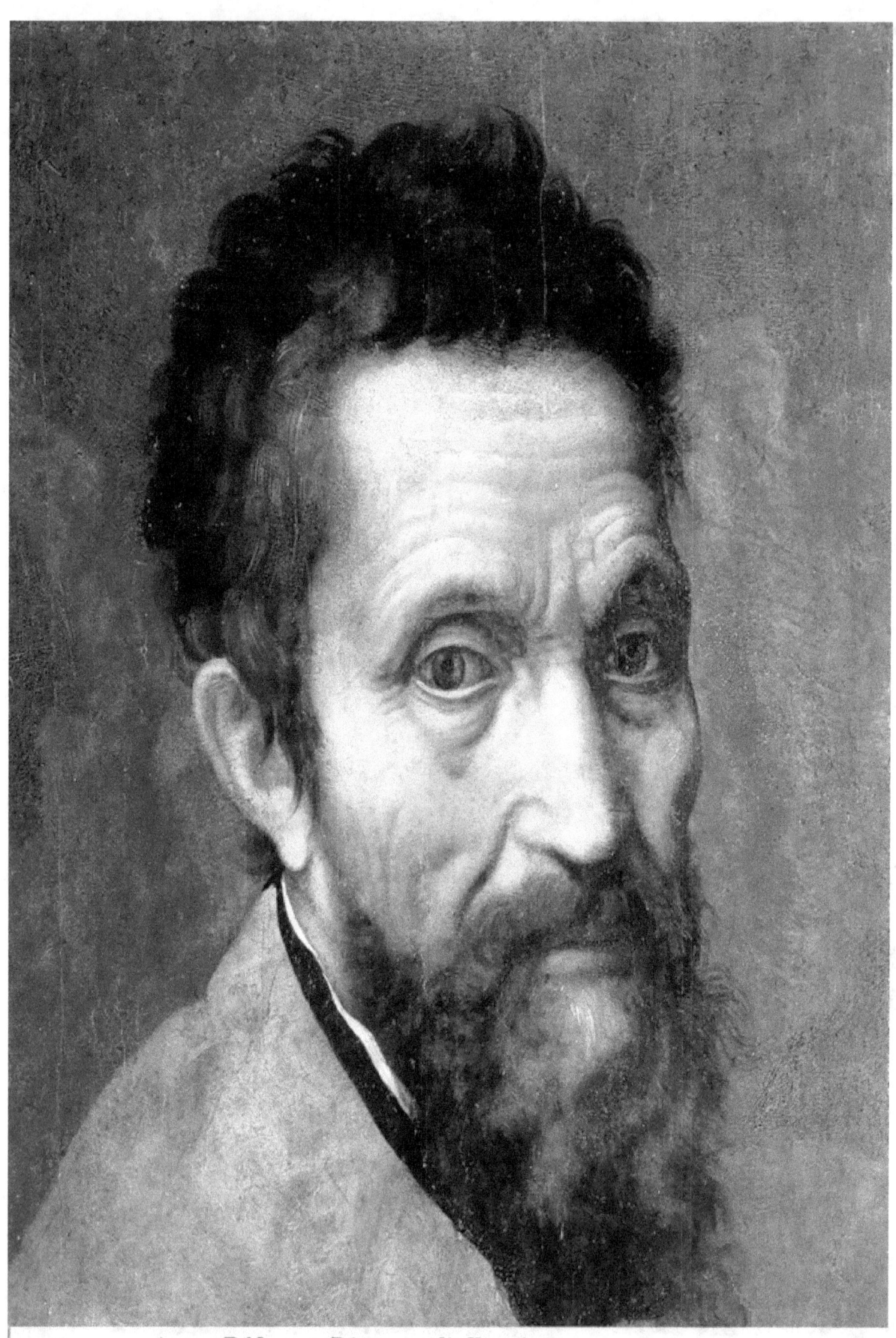

MICHELANGELO BUONARROTI (1475-1564) Italy

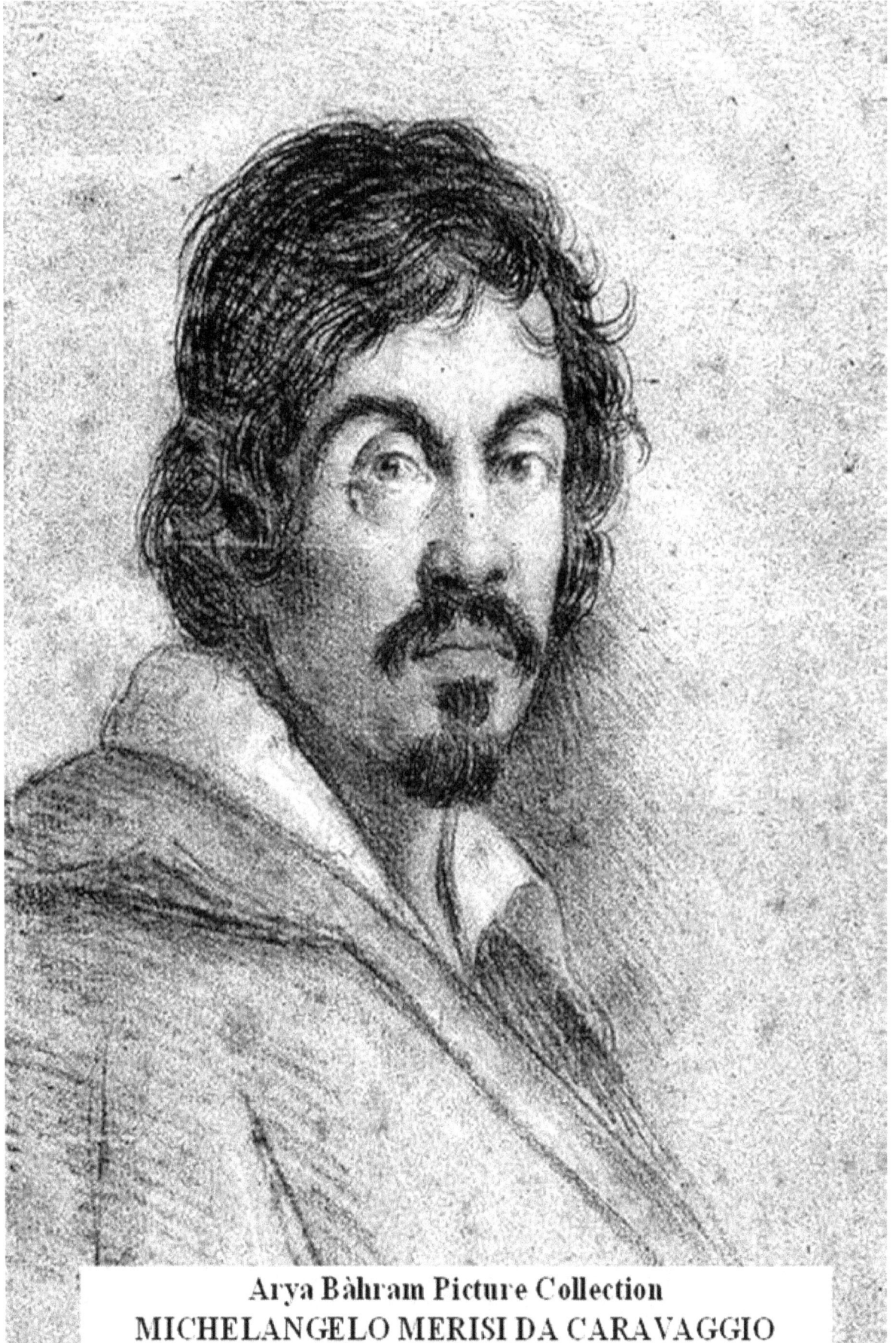

Arya Bàhram Picture Collection
MICHELANGELO MERISI DA CARAVAGGIO
(1571-1610) Italy

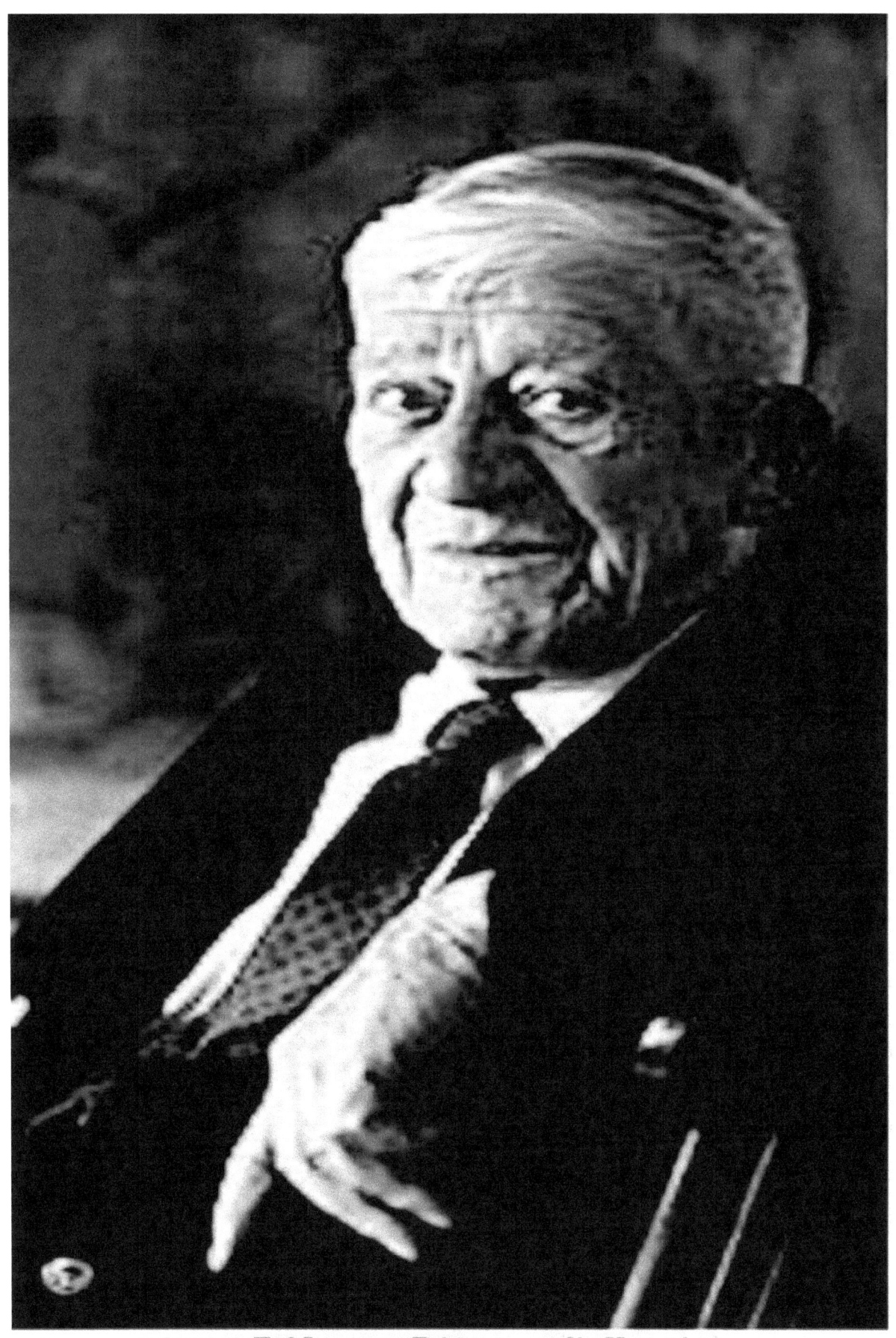

OSKAR KOKOSCHKA (1886 – 1980) Austria

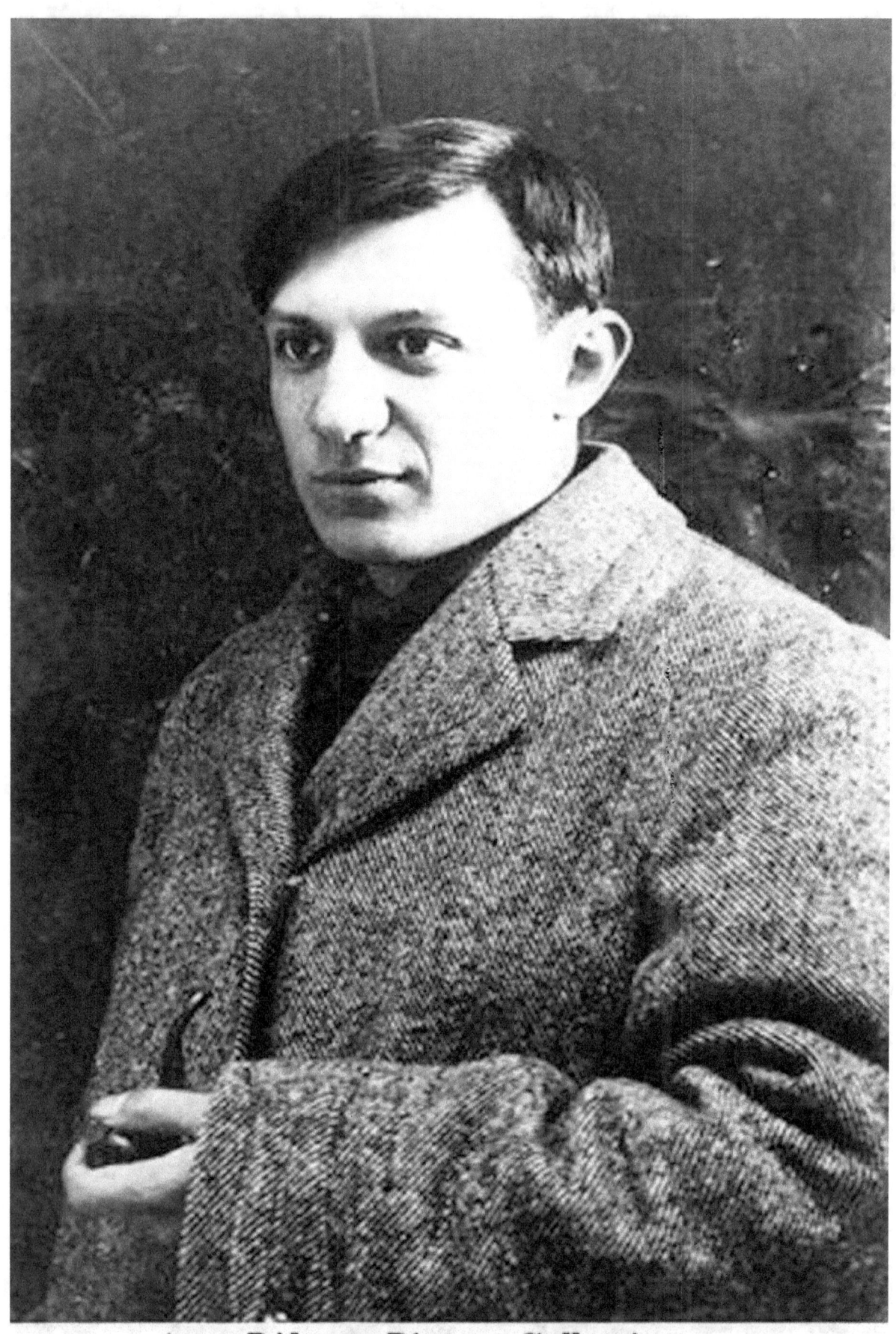

Arya Bàhram Picture Collection
PABLO PICASSO (1881-1973) Spain

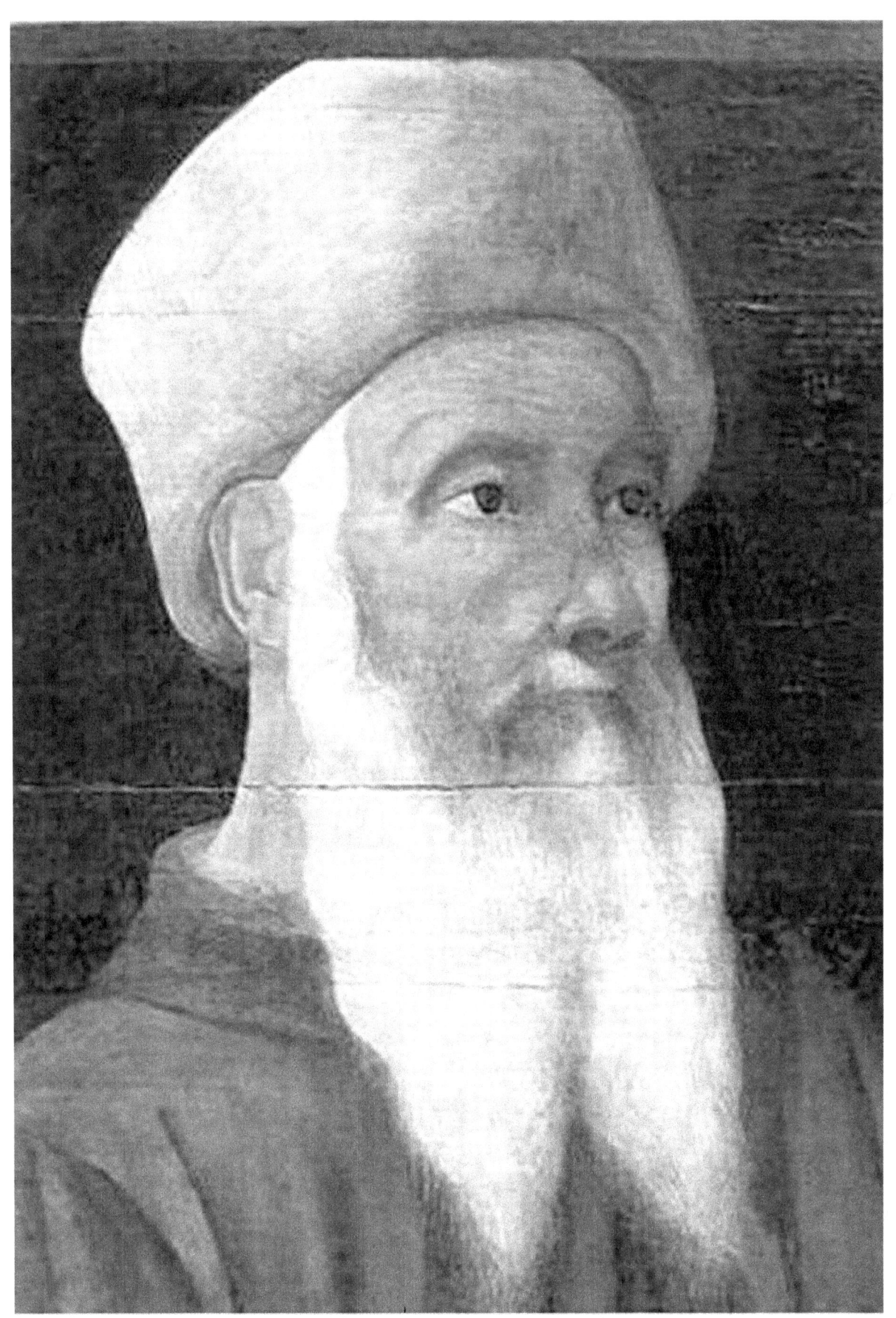

Arya Bàhram Picture Collection
PAOLO UCCELLO (1397-1475) Italy

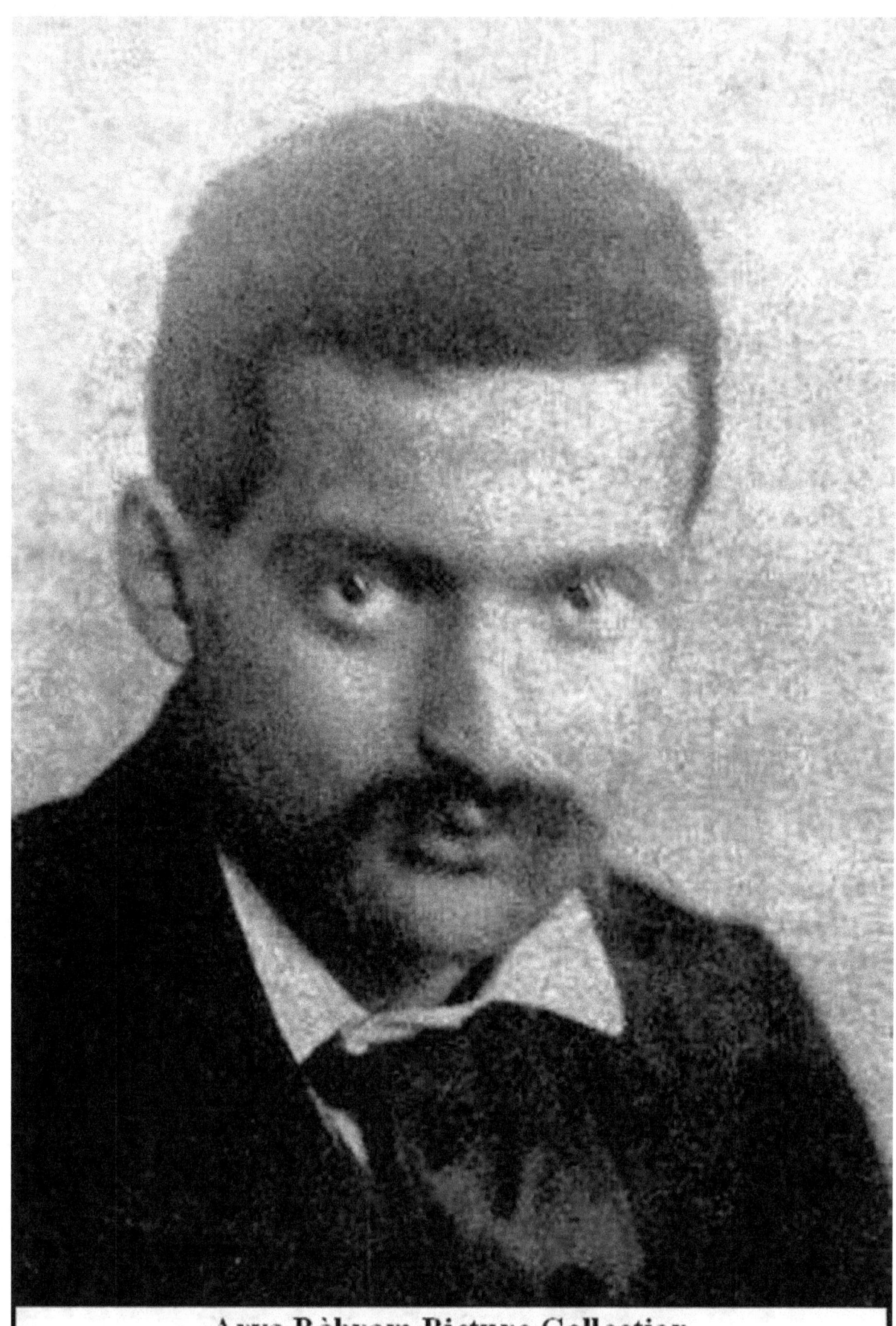

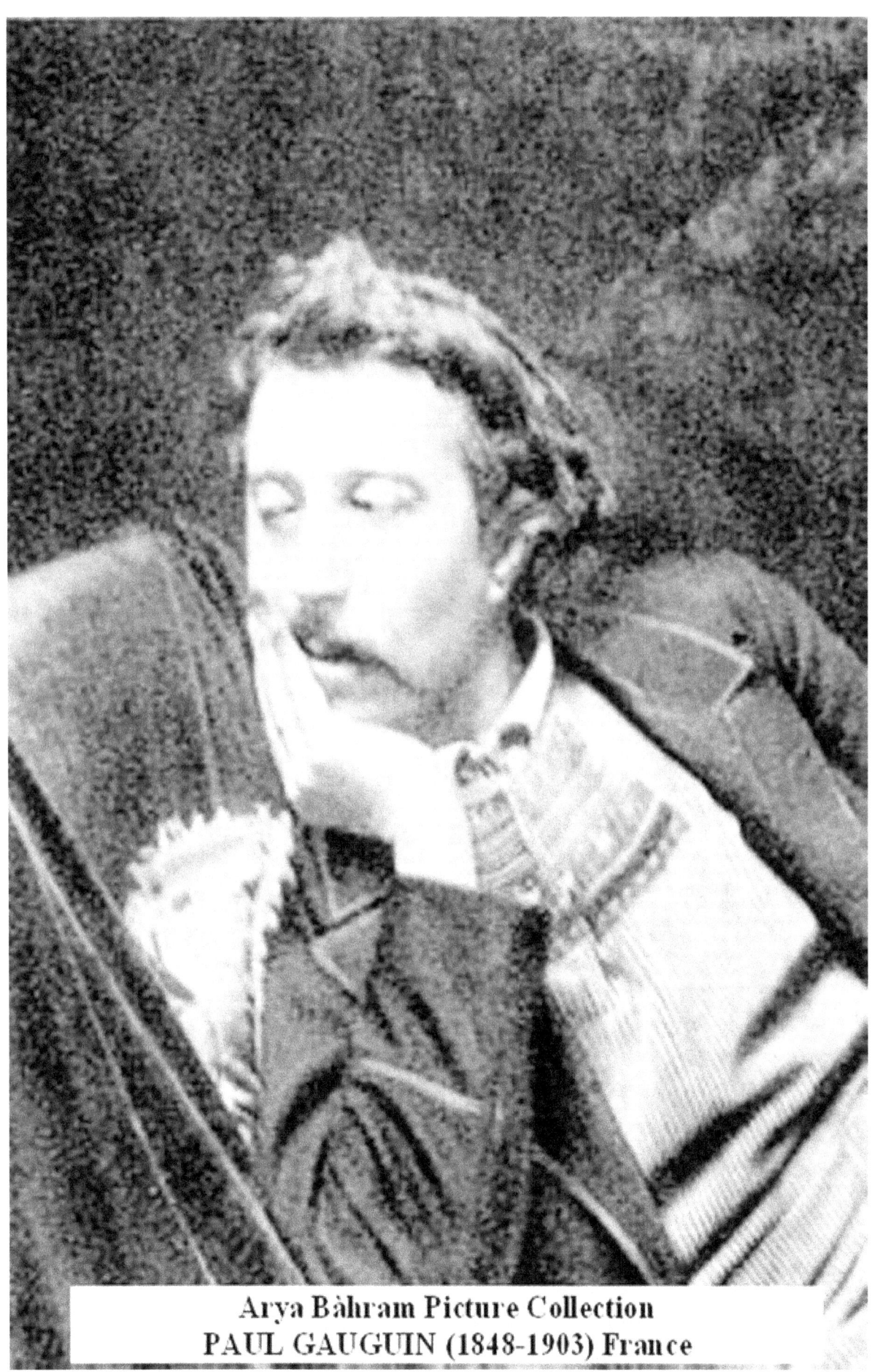

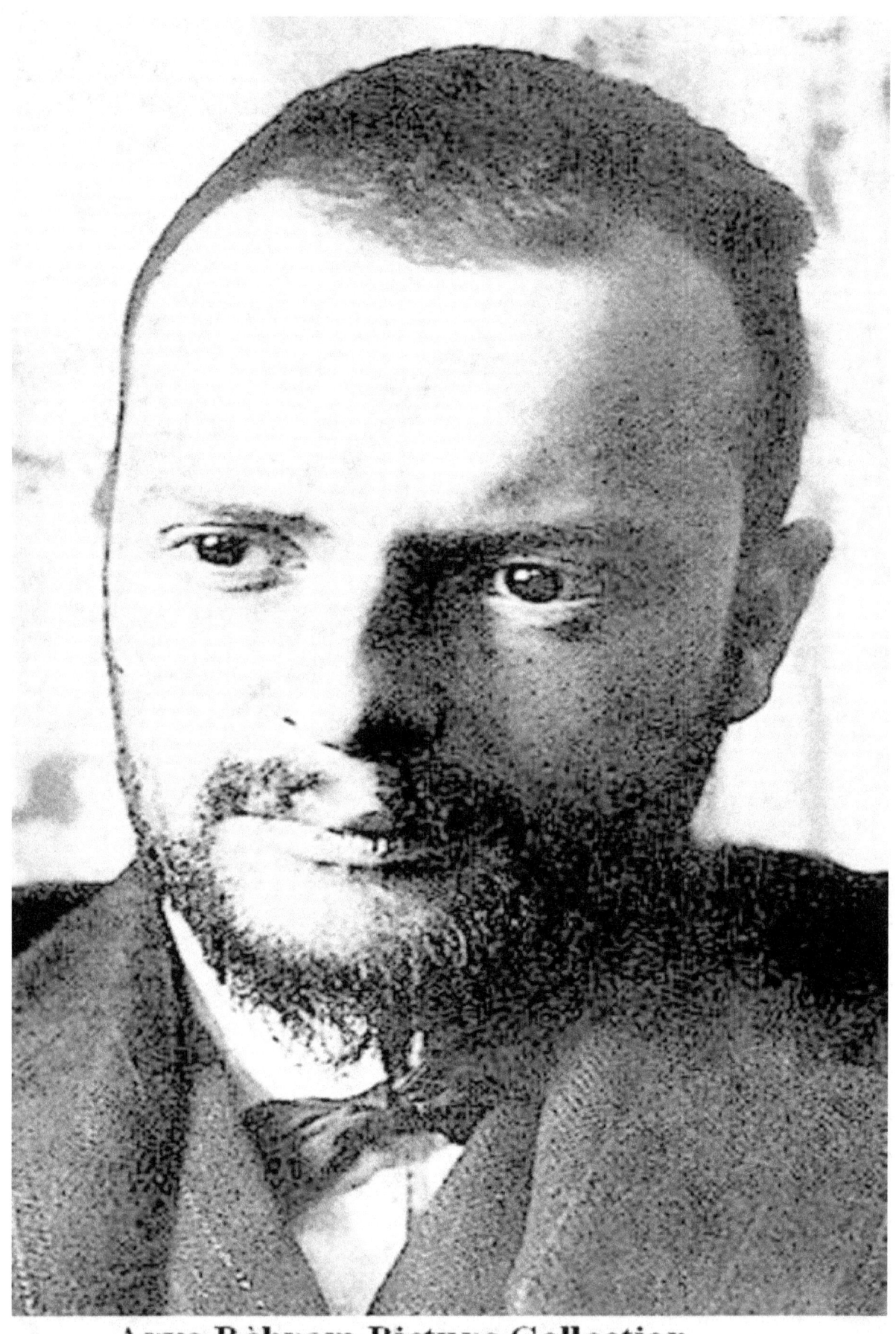

Arya Bàhram Picture Collection
PAUL KLEE (1879-1940) Switzerland

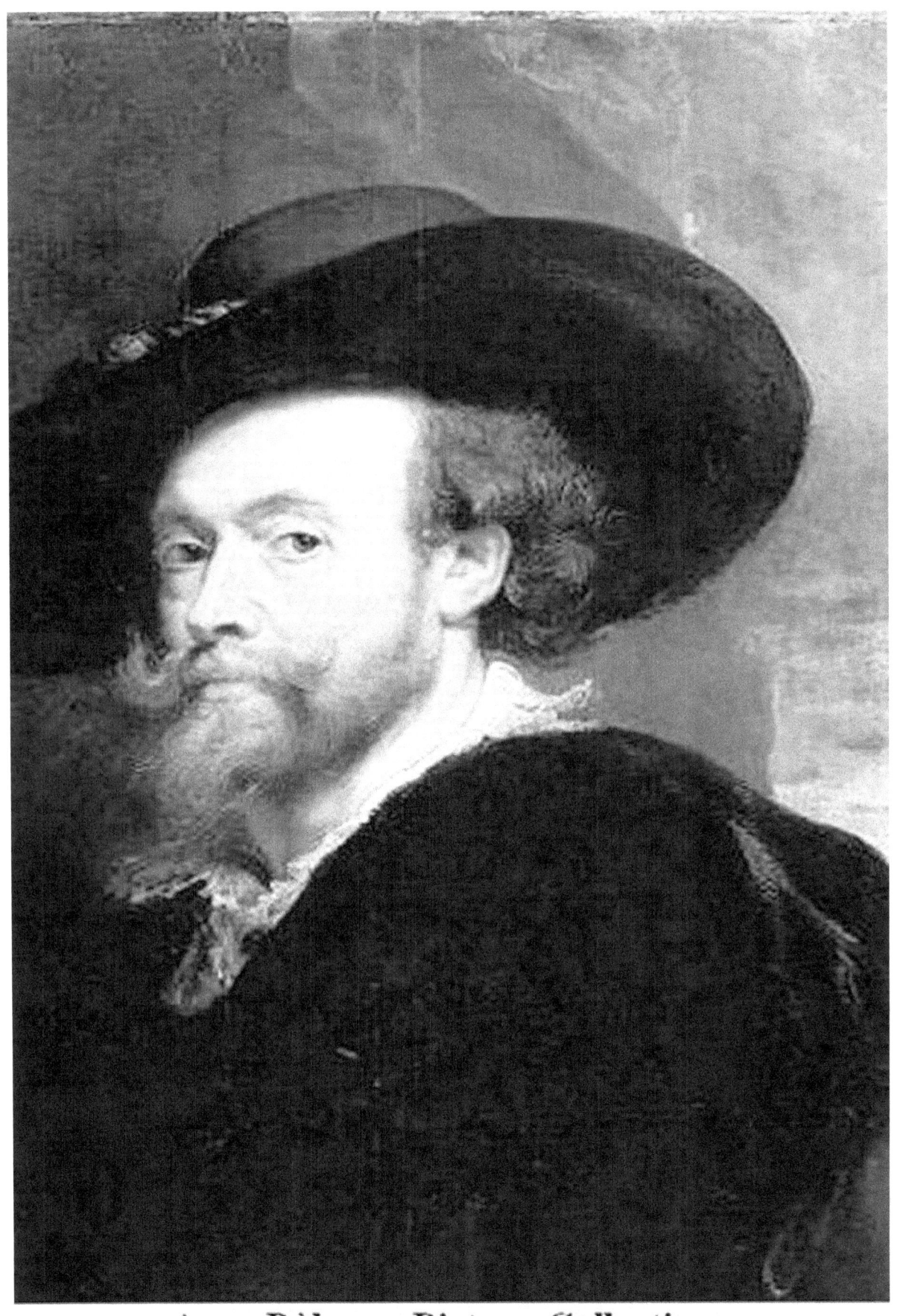

PETER PAUL RUBENS (1577-1640) Netherland

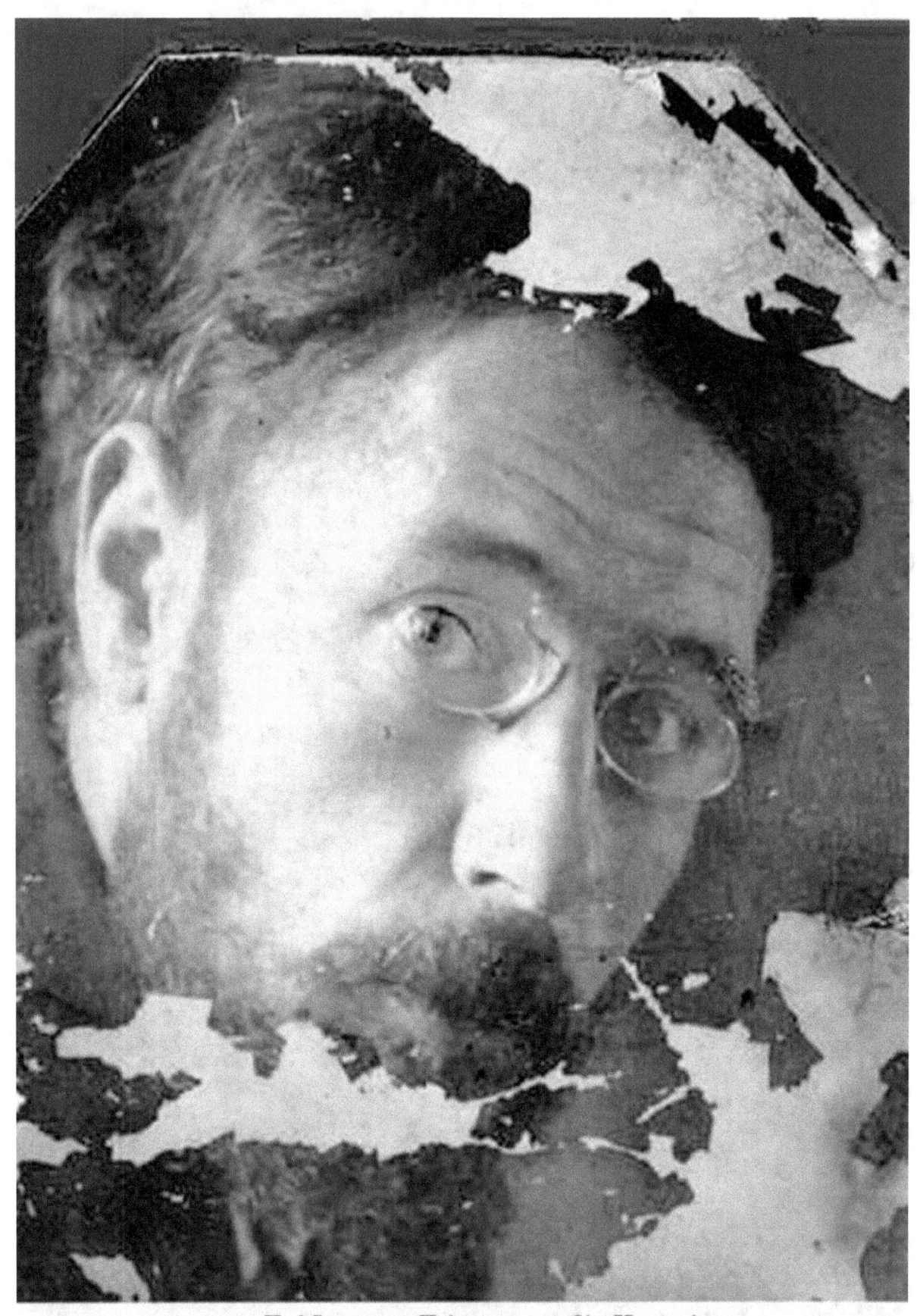

Arya Bàhram Picture Collection
PIERRE BONNARD (1867-1947) France

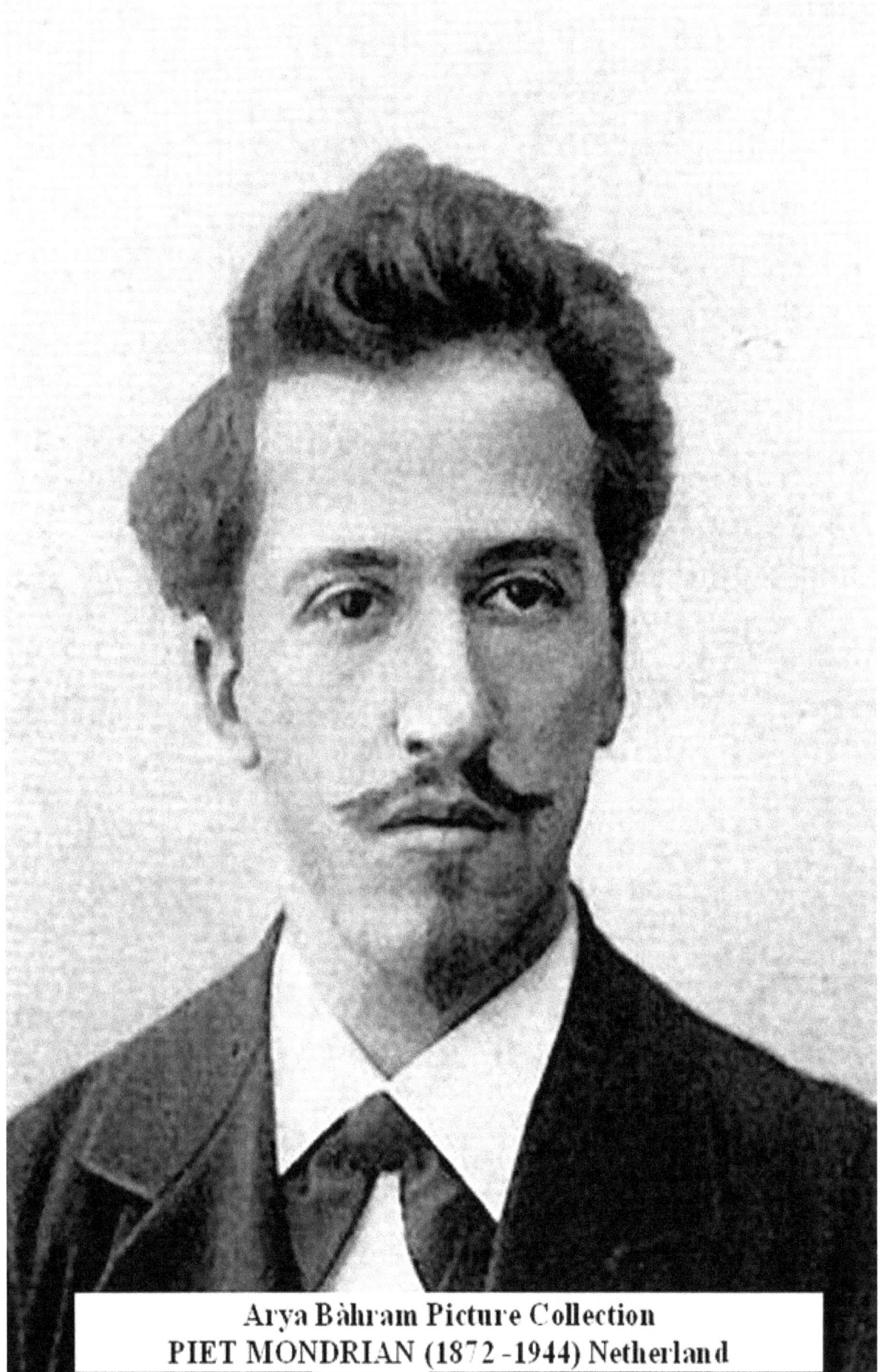

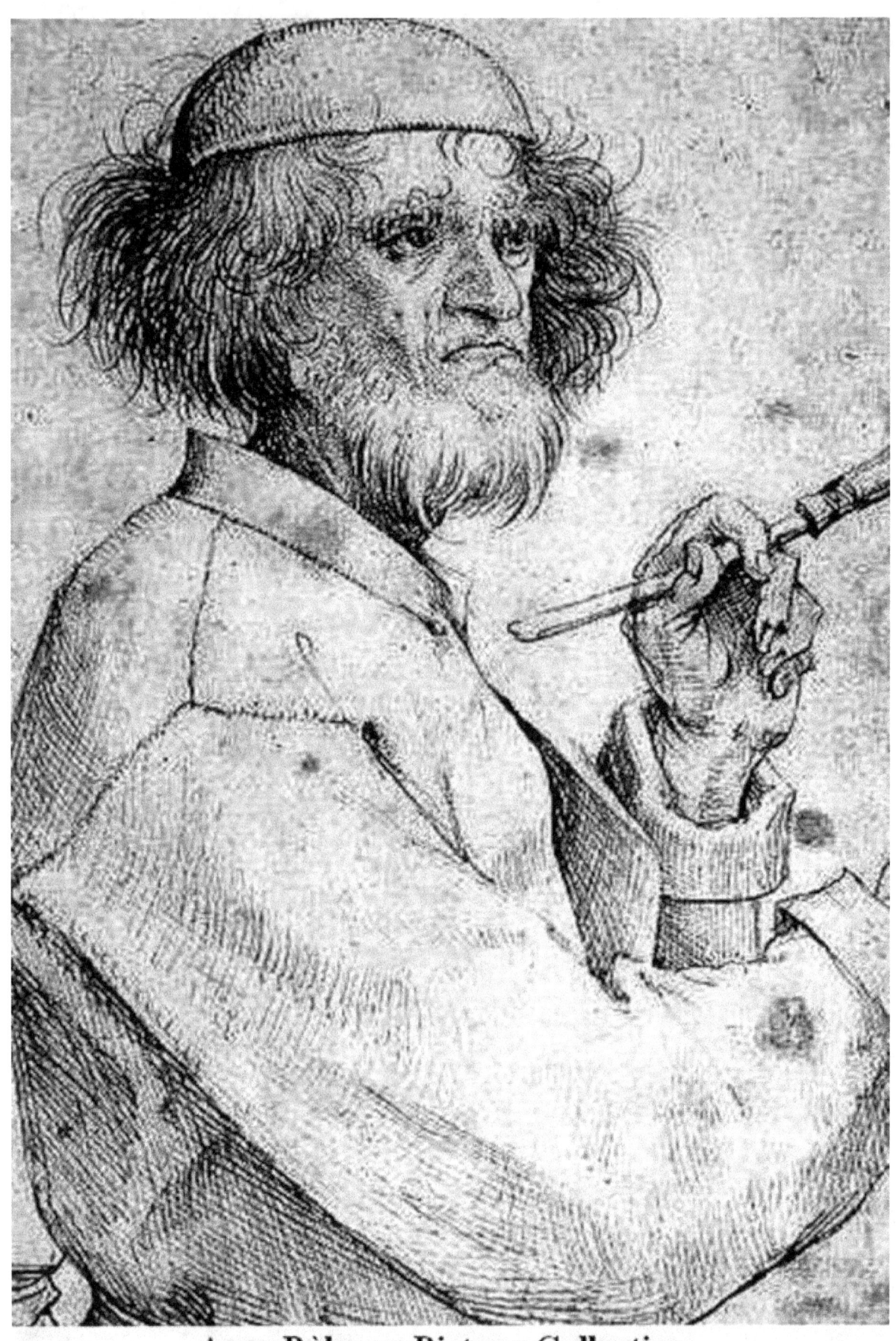

PIETER BRUEGEL THE ELDER (1528-1569) Belgium

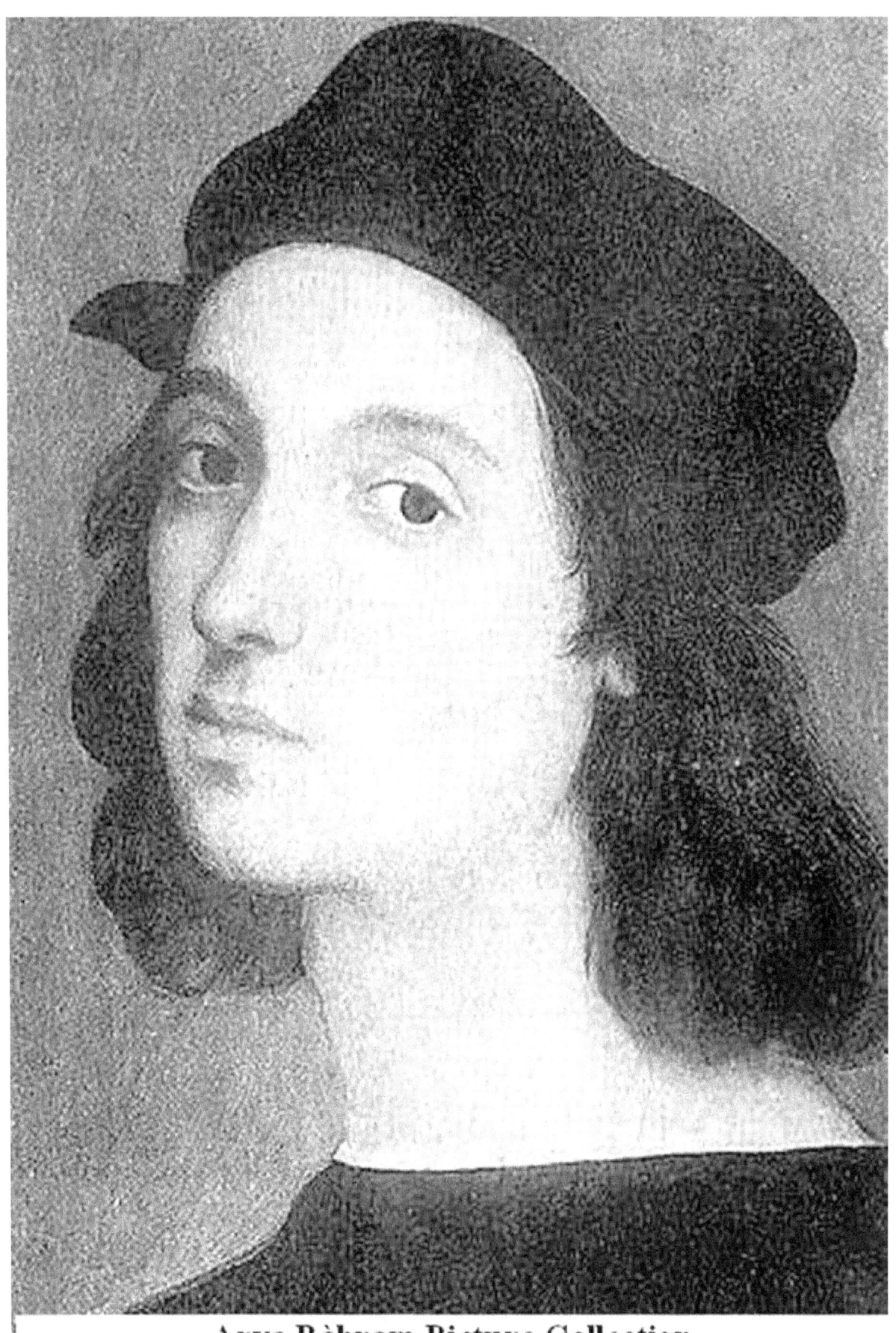

Arya Bàhram Picture Collection
RAPHAEL (1483-1520) Italy

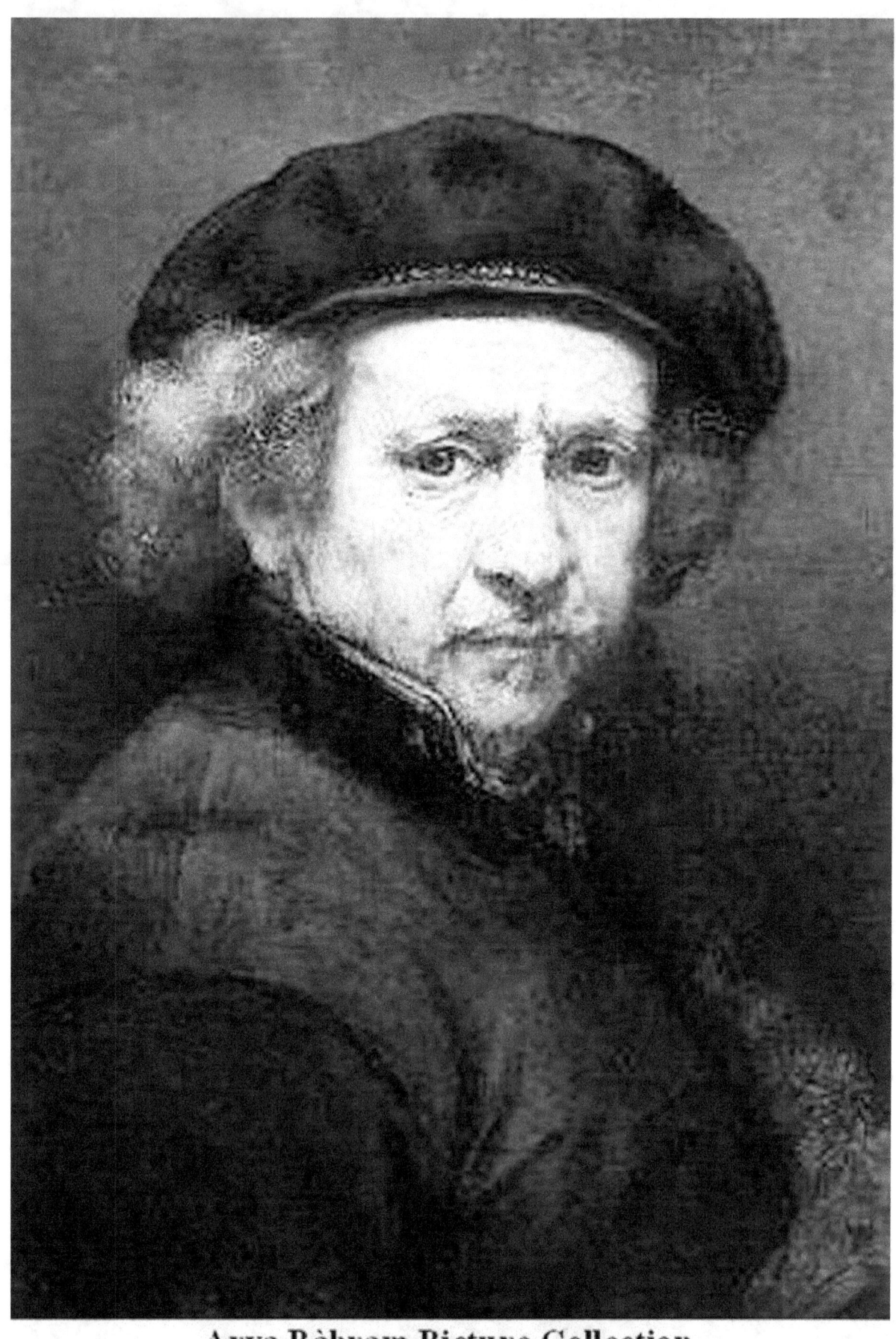

Arya Bàhram Picture Collection
REMBRANDT VAN RIJN (1606–1669) Netherland

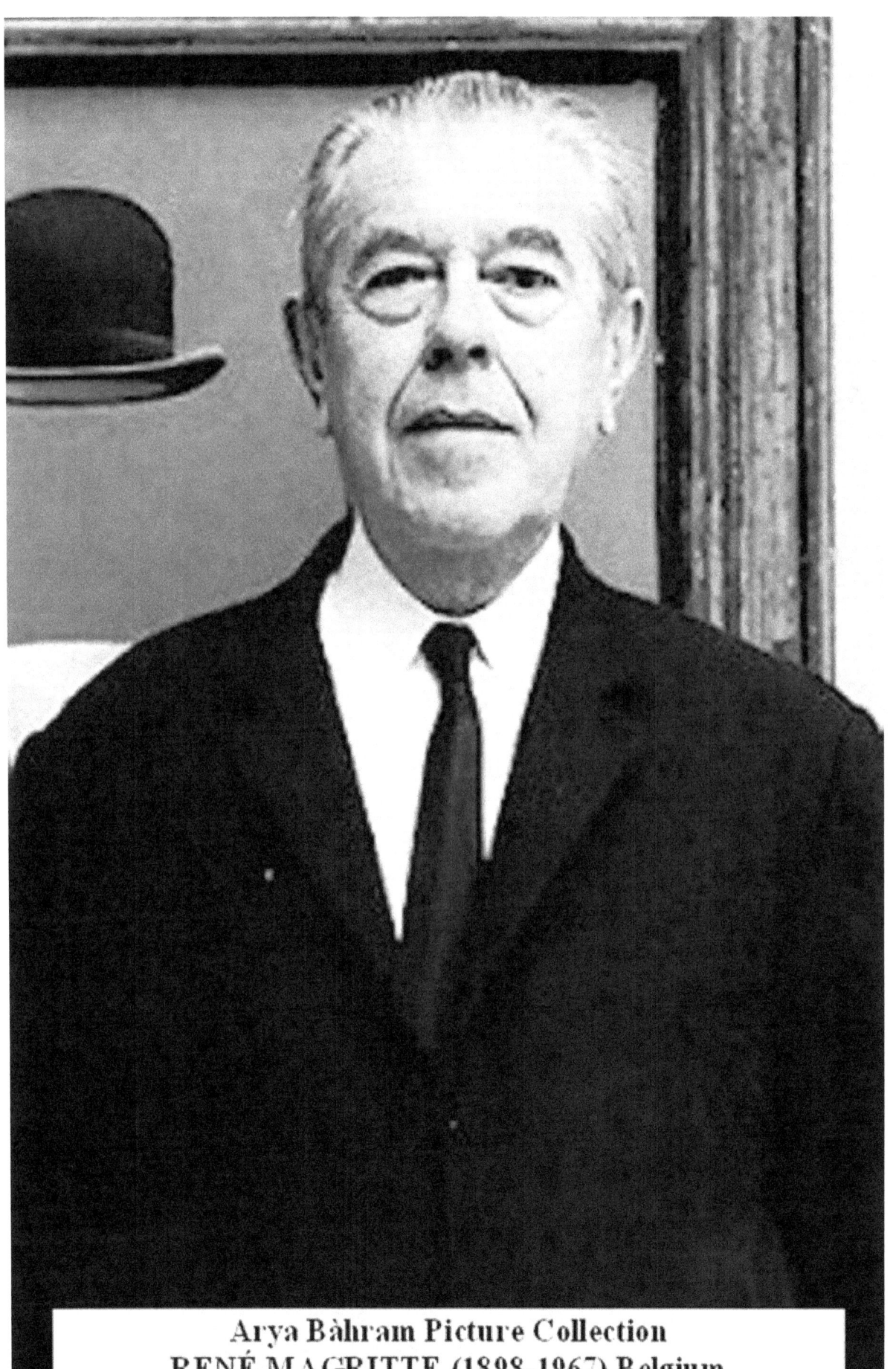

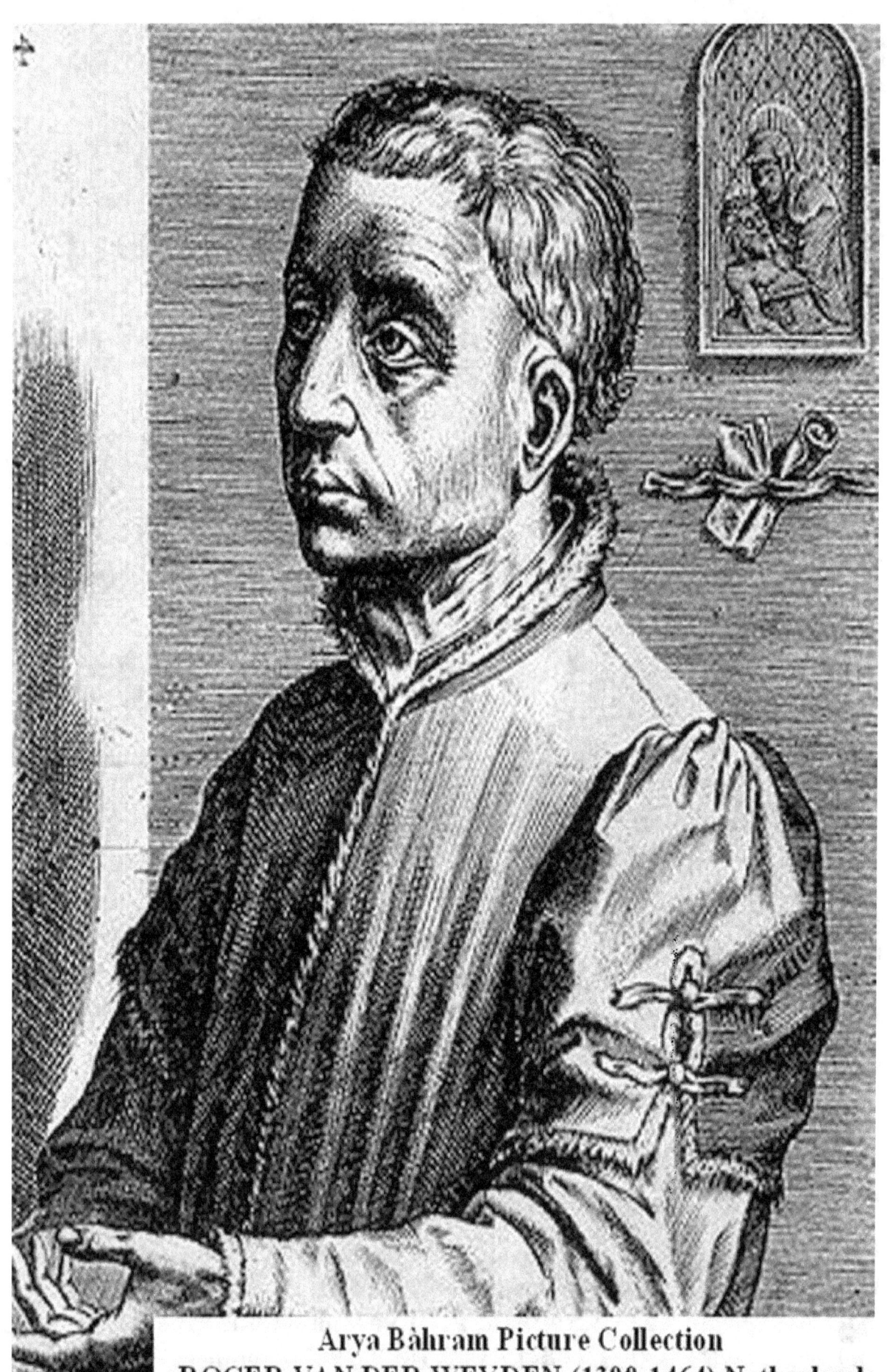

ROGER VAN DER WEYDEN (1399-1464) Netherland

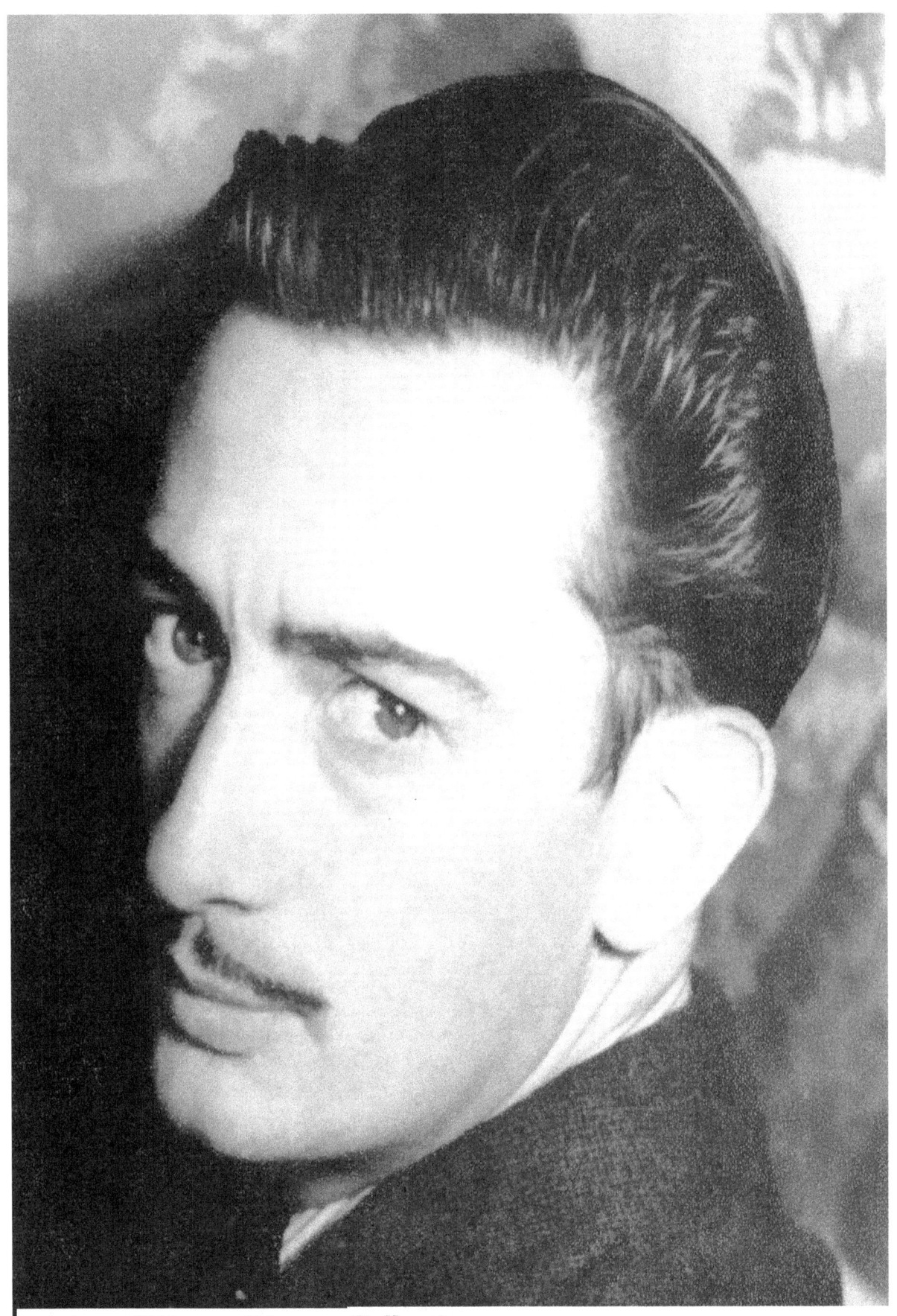

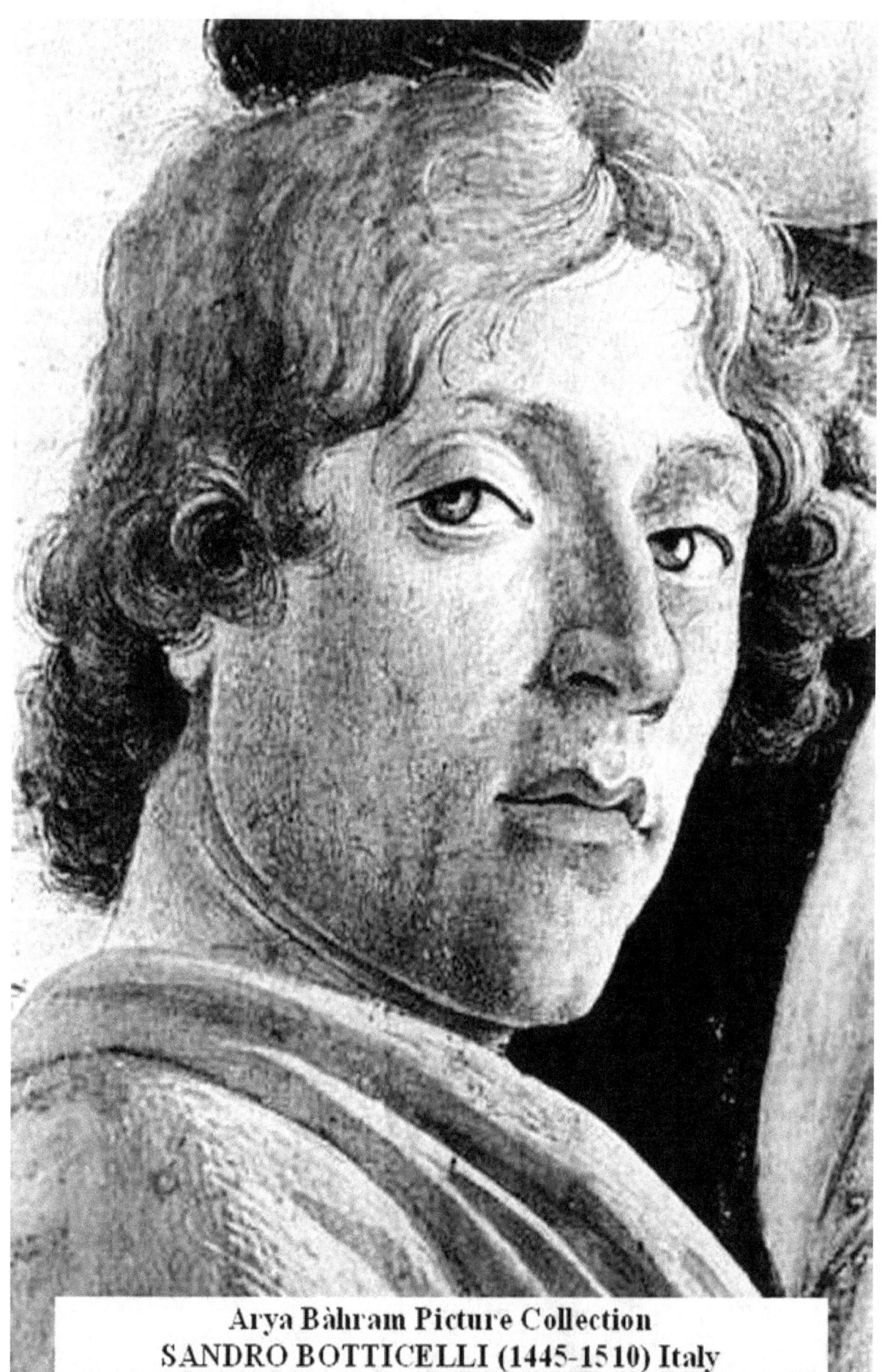

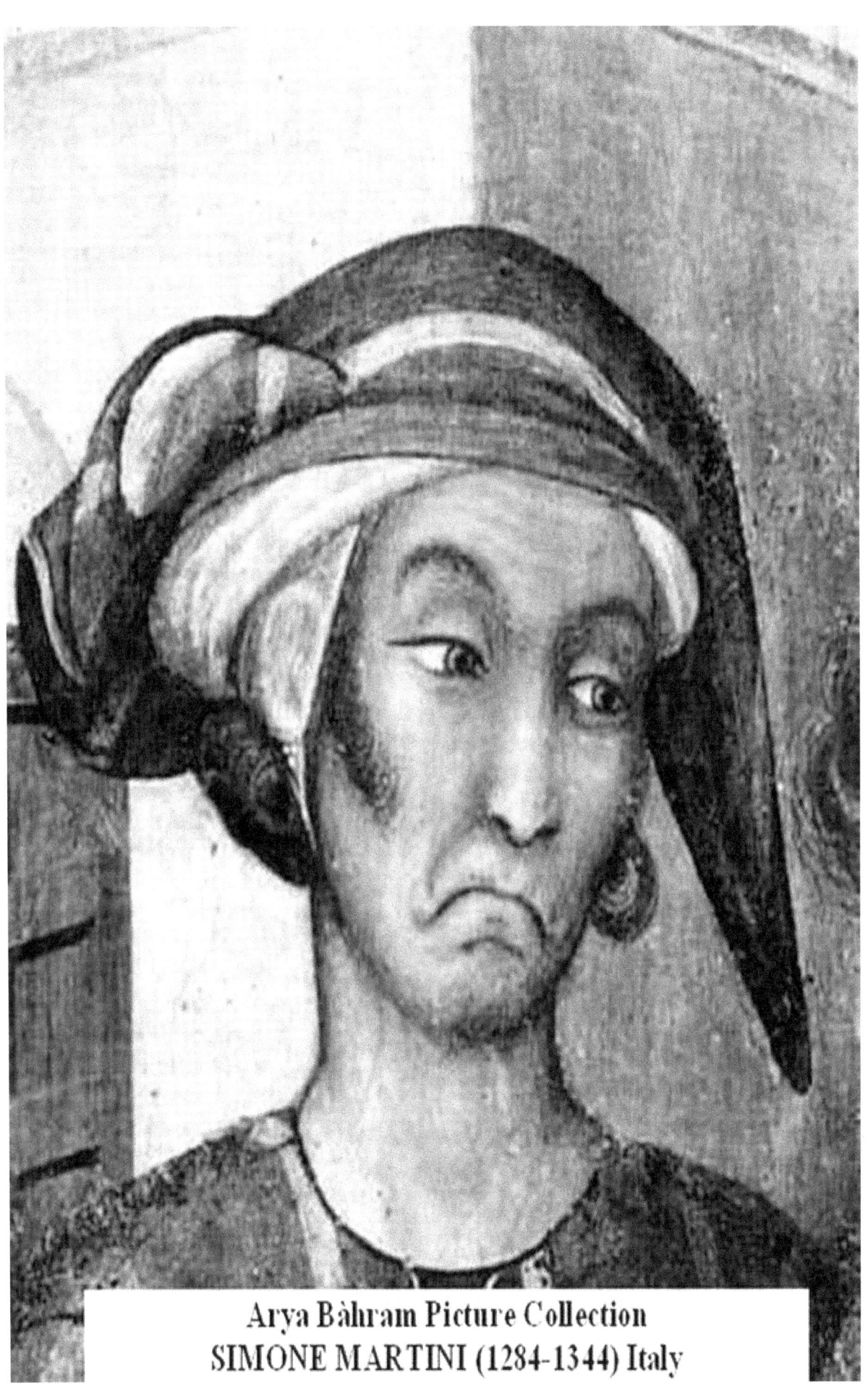

SIMONE MARTINI (1284-1344) Italy

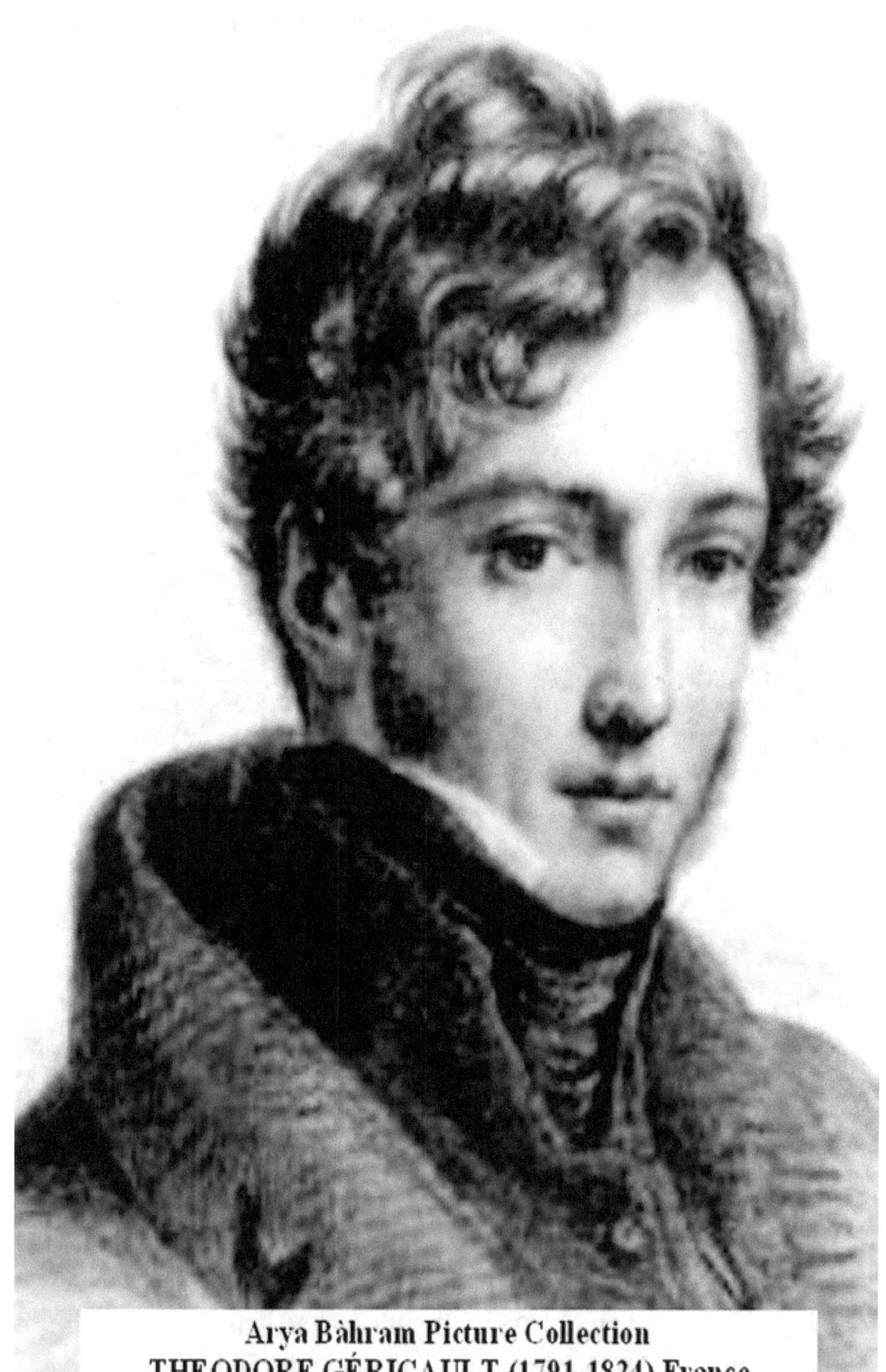

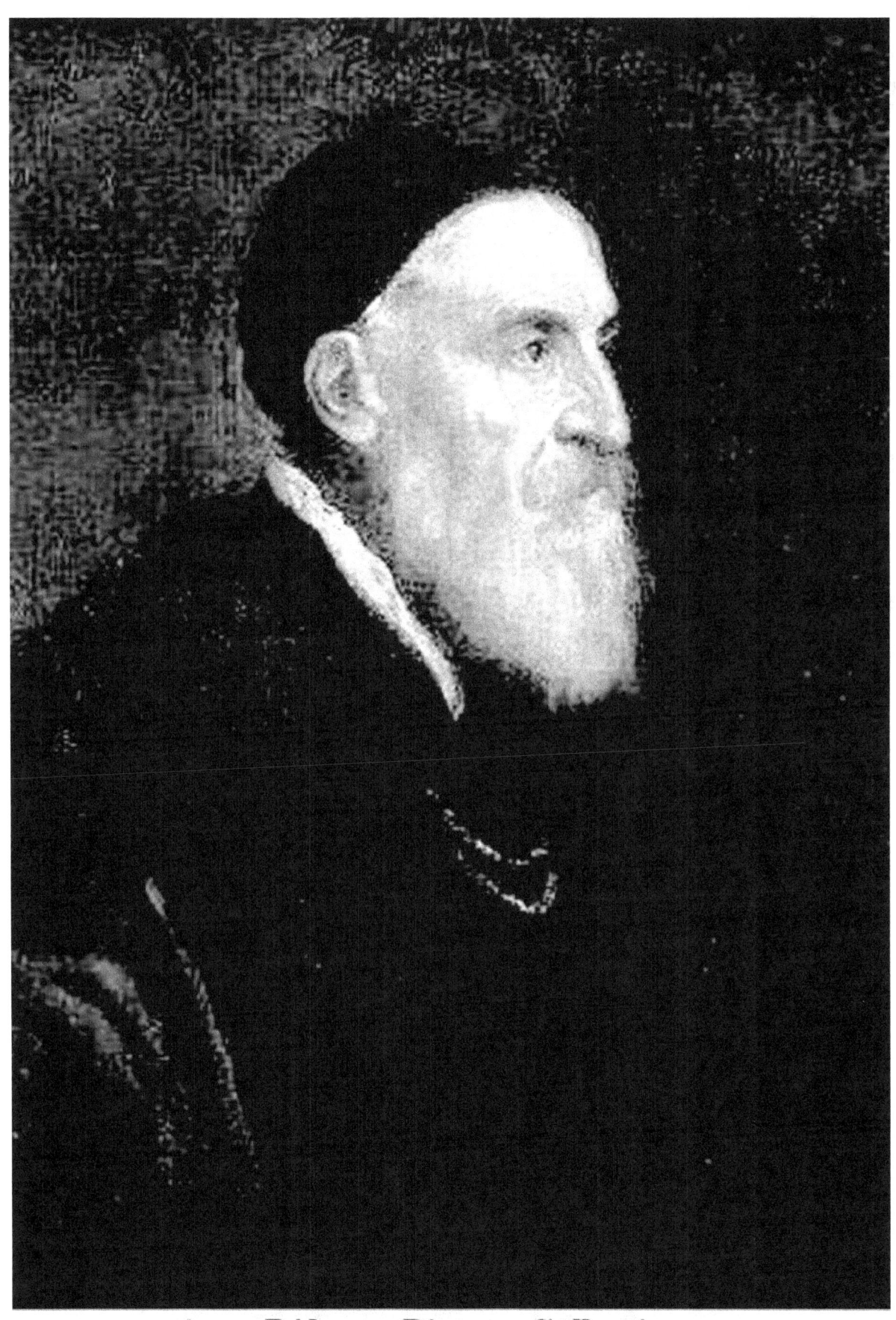

Arya Bàhram Picture Collection
TIZIANO VECELLIO (c.1476-1576) Italy

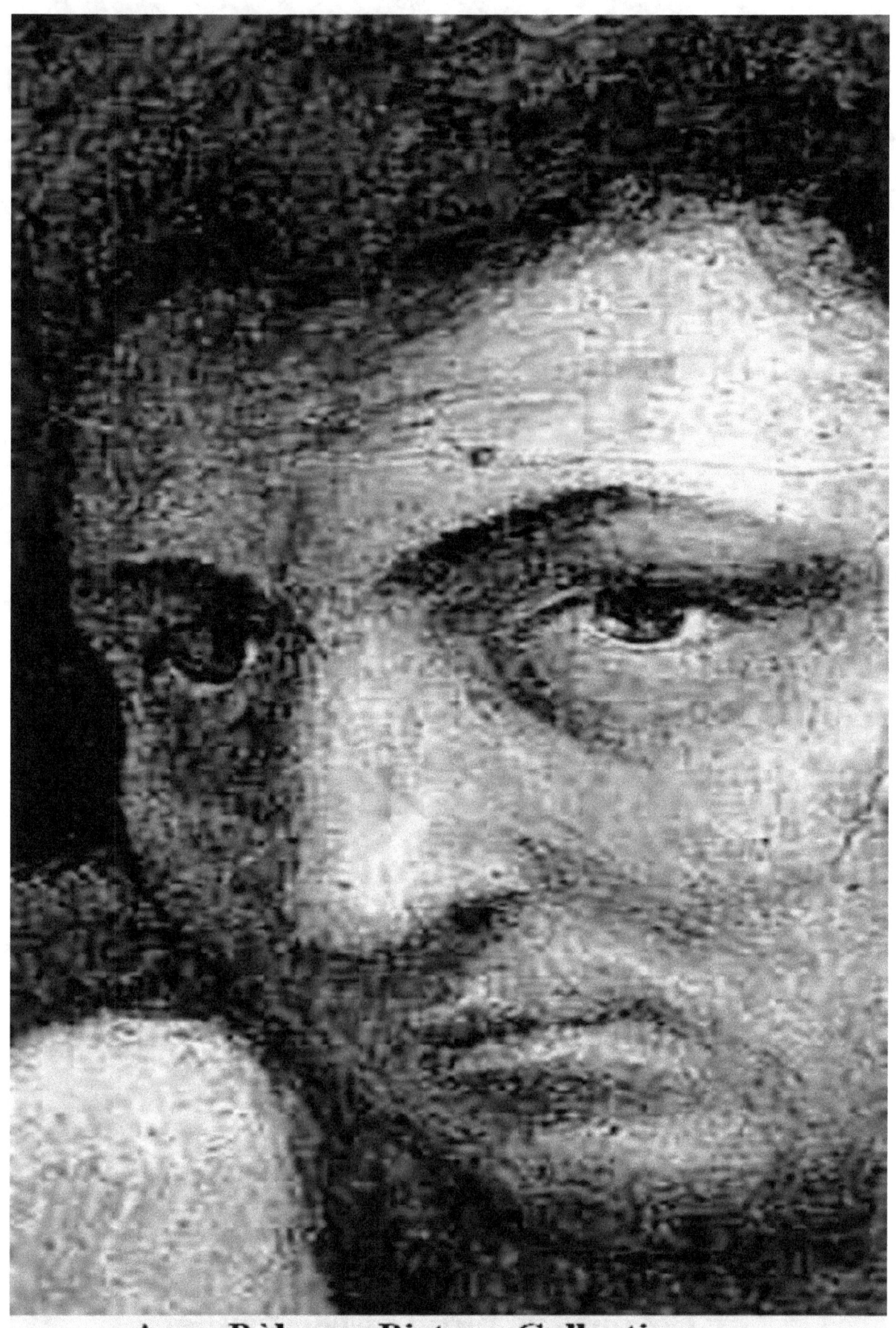

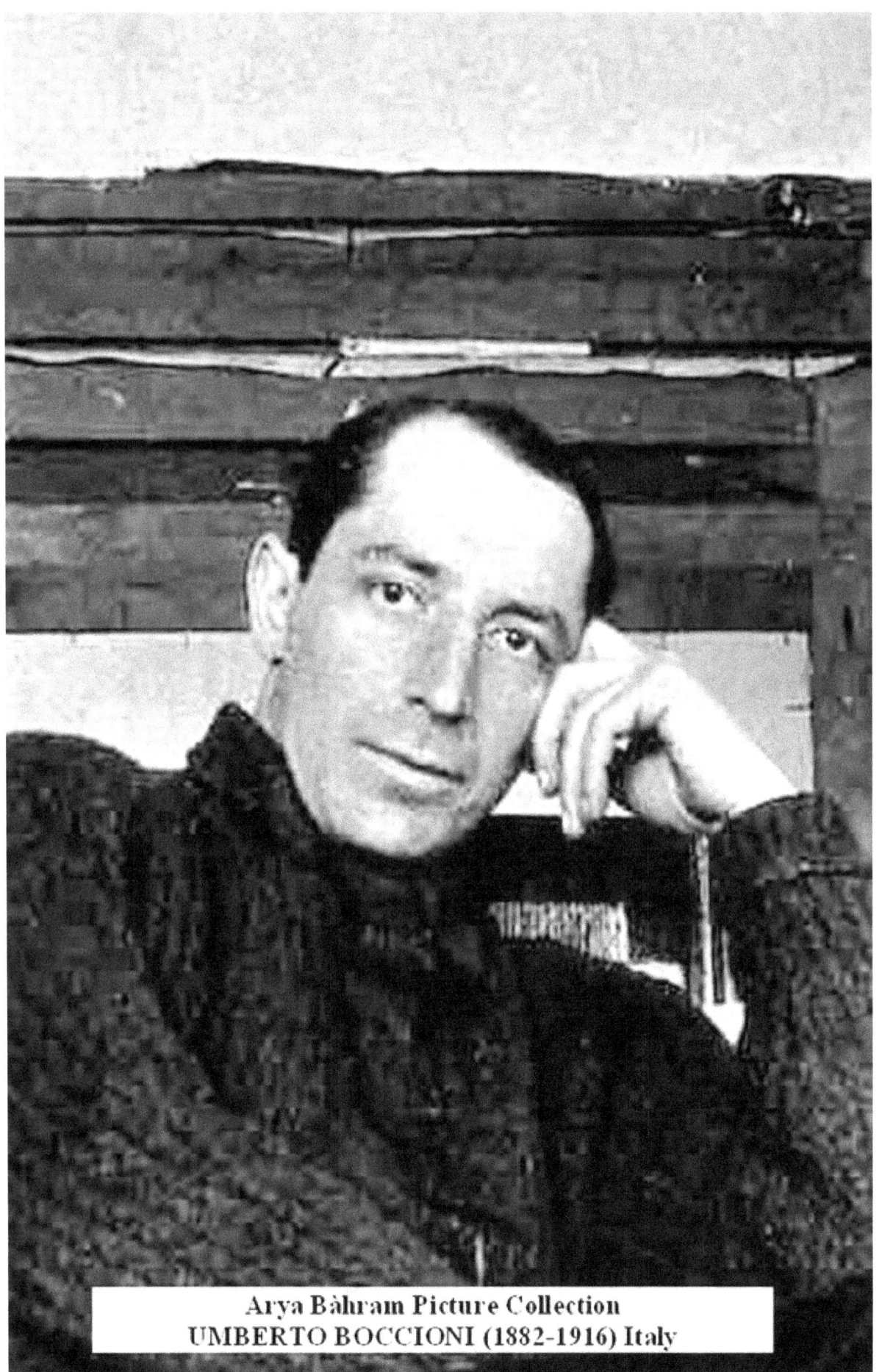

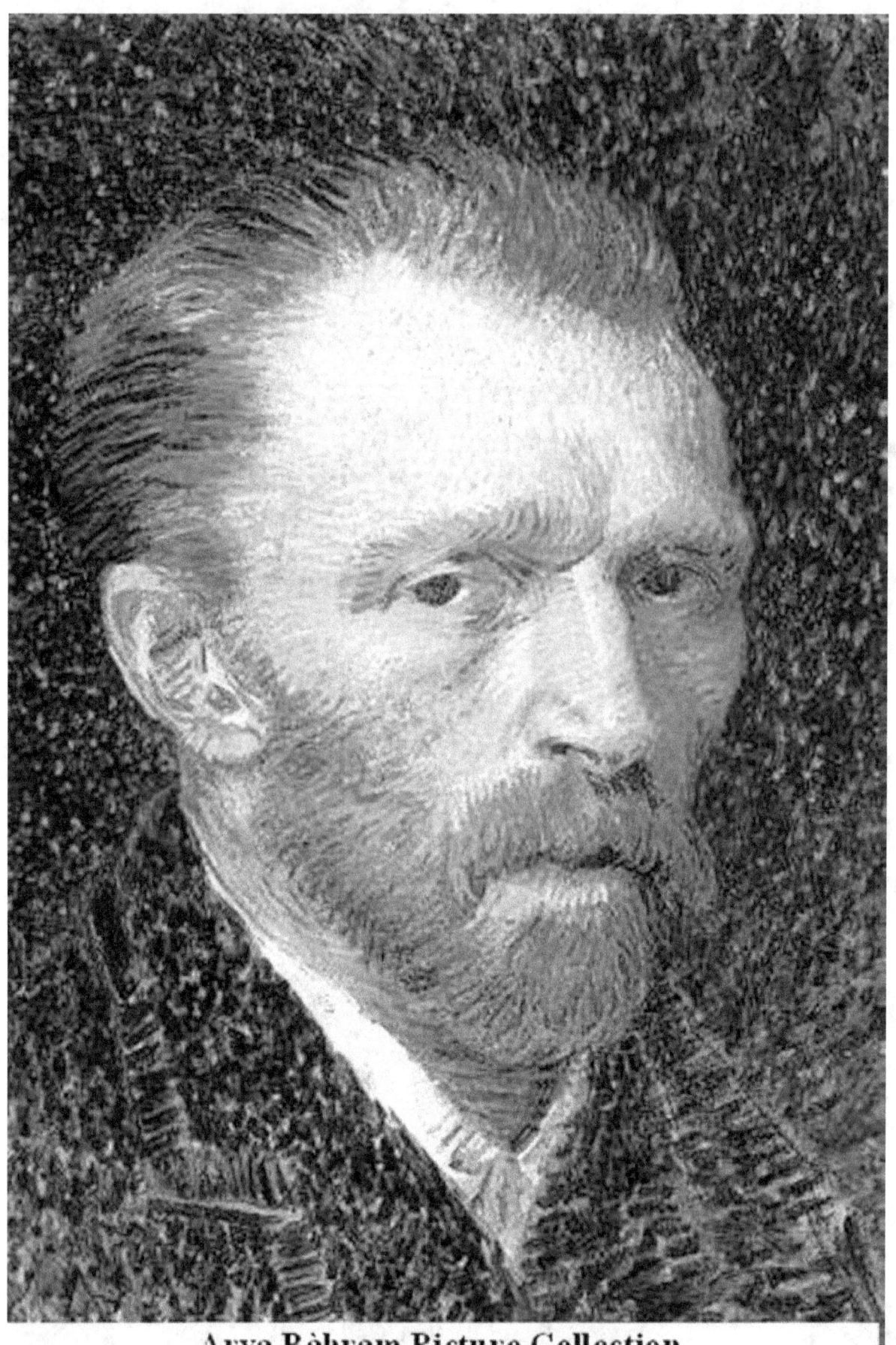

Arya Bàhram Picture Collection
VINCENT VAN GOGH (1853-1890) Netherland

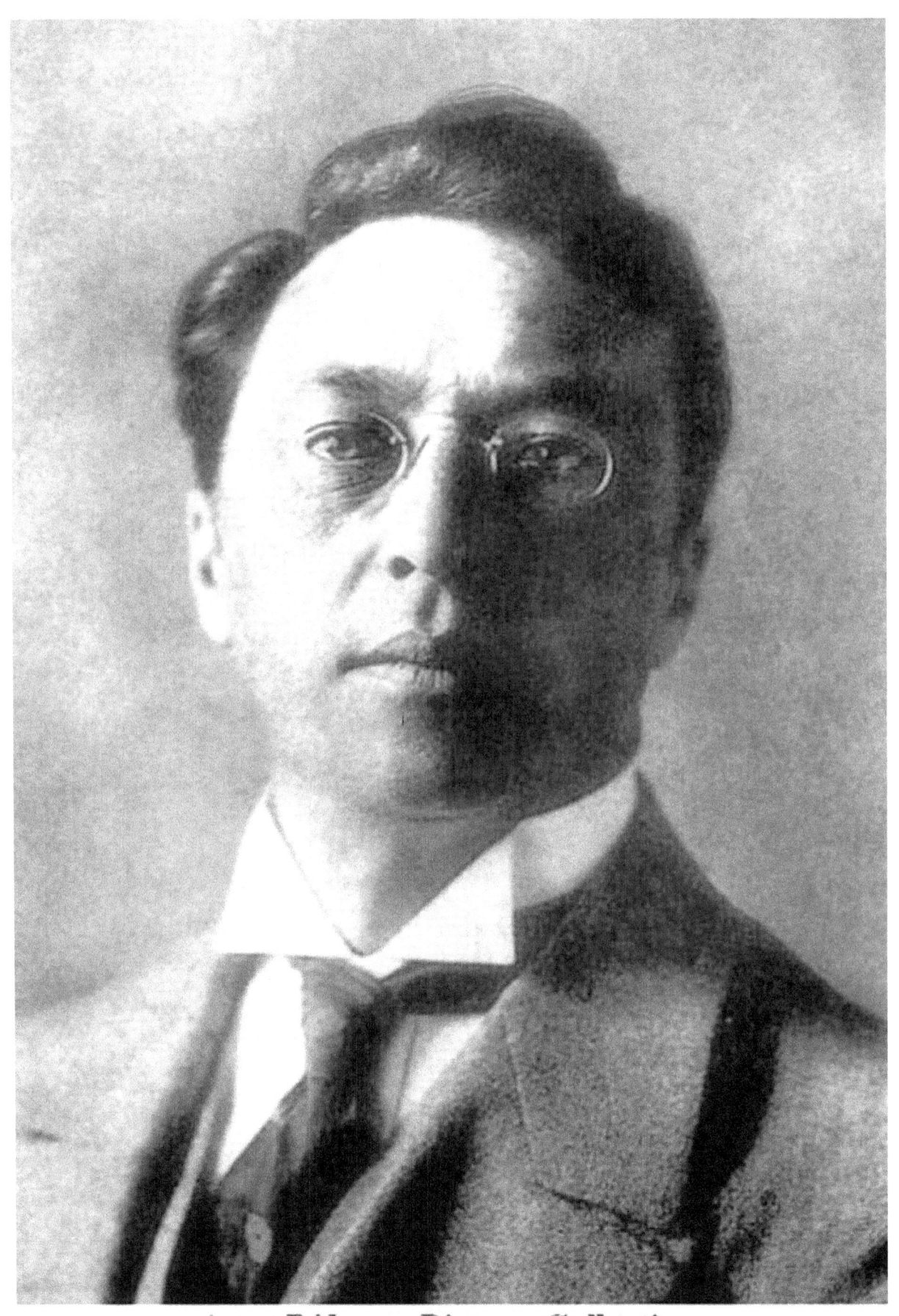

WASSILY KANDINSKY (1866-1944) Russia

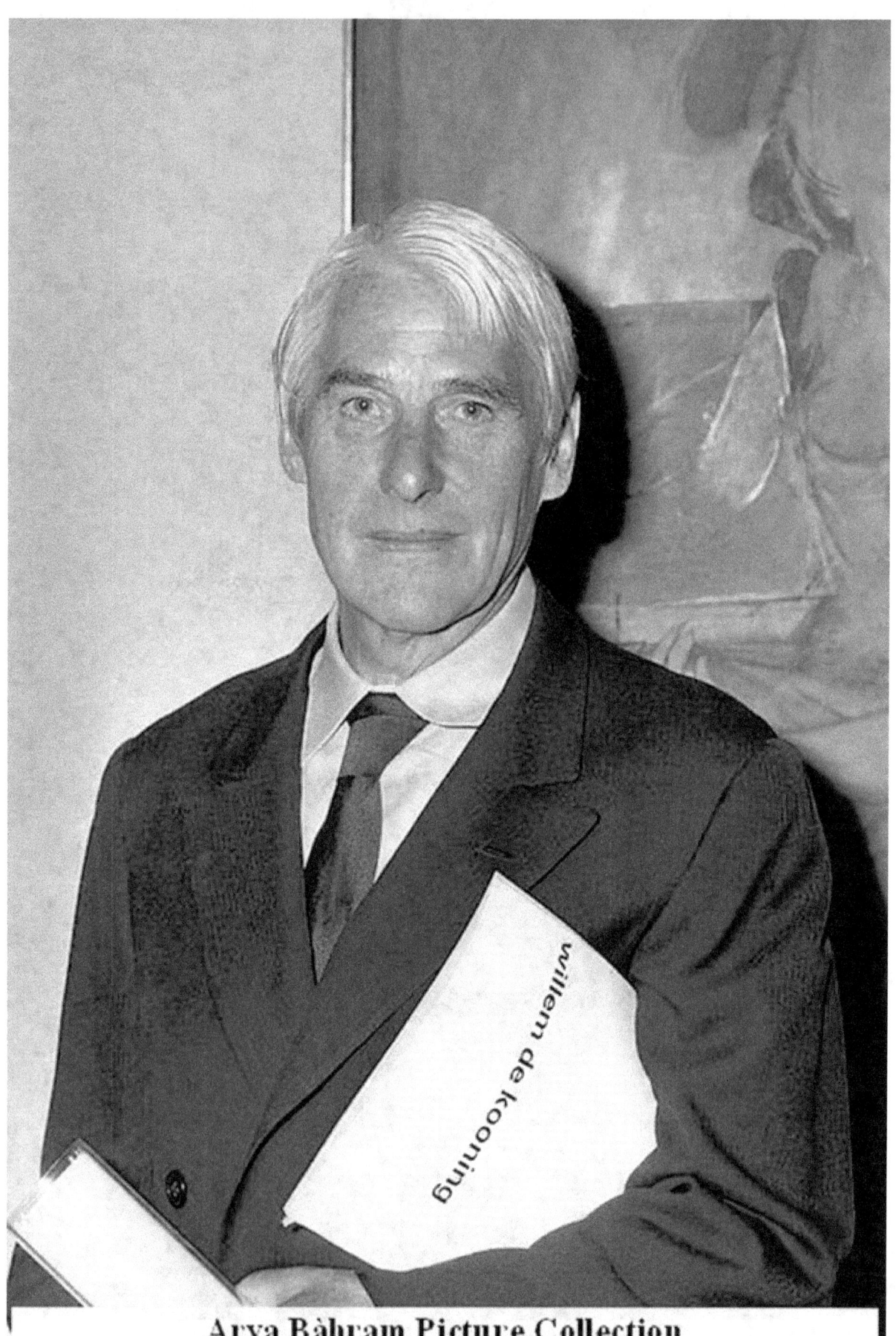

willem de koooning

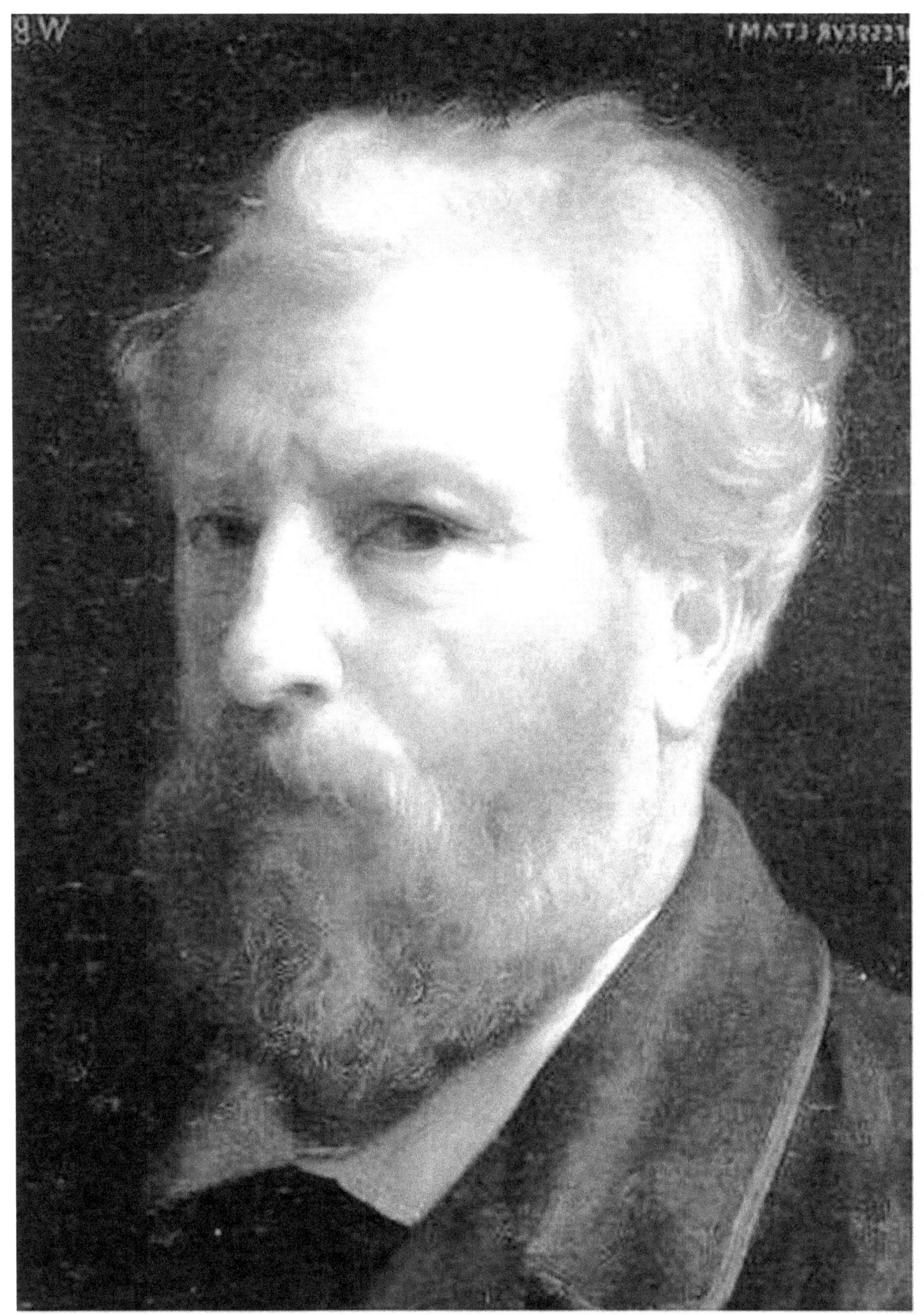

Arya Bàhram Picture Collection
WILLIAM ADOLPHE BOUGUEREAU (1825-1905)
France

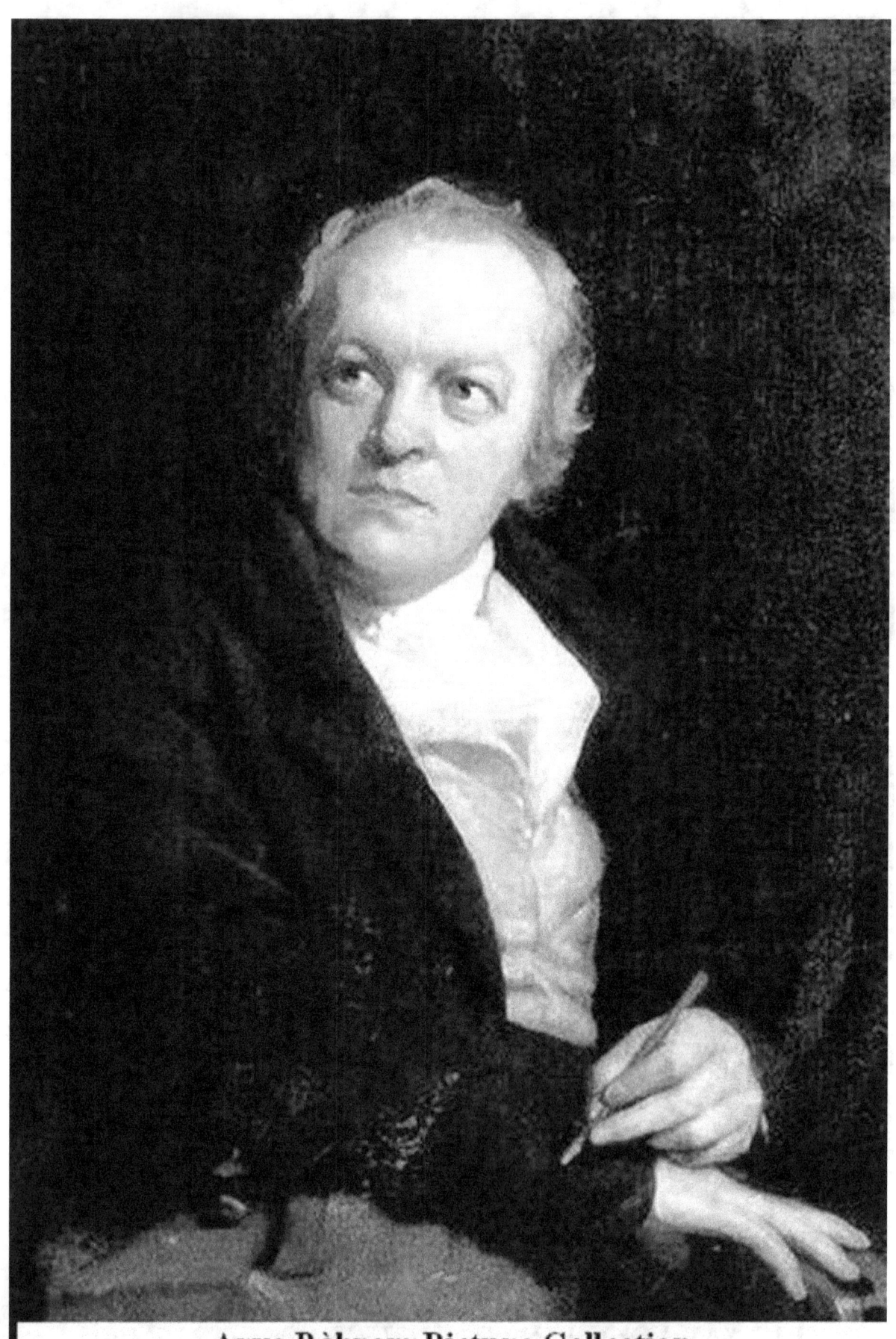

Arya Bàhram Picture Collection
WILLIAM BLAKE (1757-1827) England

www.ingramcontent.com/pod-product-compliance
Lightning Source LLC
Chambersburg PA
CBHW060009210526
45170CB00017B/2119